PROFESSIONAL TRADING SYSTEM

Published by Windsor Books

P.O. Box 280

Brightwaters, N.Y., 11718

Manufactured in the United States of America

About the Author

R. C. ALLEN

The author of this book, R. C. Allen, has been associated with commodity trading for more than thirty years. And he has developed good relationship with hundreds of traders in every area of the United States, Canada and London, England.

He is the originator and developer of the 4 day, 9 day and 18 day moving averages in 1971 and printed in January, 1972. This commodity trend indicator together with his "Precision Timing Tool" helps to make the trading of commodities more accurate and more profitable.

This "Professional Trading System" is now so well received that it is used by thousands of traders and large commercial interests and is one of the tools printed each week on the pages of three of the largest Chart Services in the United States.

In 1955, Mr. Allen was the first man to point out, on a nationwide basis, why life insurance stocks offer an unusual opportunity for large capital gains. His interesting, fact filled book, "How To Build A Fortune And Save On Taxes" opened the eyes to several million people to the unusual potential for profit in life insurance stocks at that time.

The above book, together with "The Truth About Life Insurance" and the special reports on life insurance policies written by Mr. Allen, helped to motivate investment-minded people to start more than six hundred new life insurance companies. Sales in those companies now total several billions of dollars in life insurance and their assets have helped to expand the economy of the United States.

Table of Contents

PREFACE

After the original printing of this book in 1972, three of the largest Commodity Chart Services in the world have included R. C. Allen's system of the Moving Averages in their chart services every week. But no clear and easy to understand explanation of the importance of the Moving Averages is given to those new subscribers who look at those charts every week.

The Moving Averages in those three charting services is based on this *Professional Trading System.*

In the past several years, it has become a standard trading guide and trading tool that many thousands of professional traders follow to help them earn more money from commodities.

We wish you luck with it also.

Sincerely,

WINDSOR BOOKS

1

THE BASIS FOR
A PROFESSIONAL TRADING SYSTEM

For those "money-conscious" traders who are unable to devote full time to the study of commodities, I believe this book can help you in two ways:

First—in the year 1971, I worked out and developed a new and improved system of "moving averages" for commodities that, in the majority of cases, can help you time your trades more carefully.

Before 1971, the three most popular averages were the 5 day average, the 9 day average and the 20 day average. I studied those averages very carefully. After much study, analyzing and checking, I found that the timing of commodity markets can be improved if the averages are based on 4 days, 9 days and 18 days.

And, in fast-moving, high volume markets (which are the best ones to trade), the extra profits you can gain from that improved timing can give you a considerable increase in your equity.

I suggest, therefore, that you keep a record of the 4 day, 9 day and 18 day averages. If you trade in more than one contract or, if you deal in more than one commodity, the extra profits you earn are well worth the time and the effort.

The reason why the moving averages make sense is because they tend to digest all of the violent moves a market can, sometimes make, smooths them out and slowly turn a market around and get it moving—UP or DOWN in a more dependable trading pattern.

By a careful study of the "moving averages", in the way I will soon explain them, you will be able to buy back your "shorts" closer to the bottom of a move and go "long" and sell your long positions closer to the top and take profits—just before the next decline begins.

You will, of course, miss buying "on the bottom" of a move and you will also miss "selling at the top." But you will feel safer in the trades that you make and you will feel, more certain, that prices will move more persistently in your favor.

Second—I will try, through this book, to help you understand how to use these "moving averages" to earn a larger amount of profit. And, hopefully, that profit may be 300% or more every year.

And, if you can make five to seven good trades during each year, your profits, then, might be as large as 700%.

No trend and no "moving average" is perfect. But the moving averages eliminate much of the "guessing" that is done by so many traders who try to foretell what a market might be—UP or DOWN—several weeks in the future—when current news and opinions say "It is unlikely to happen."

Even the weatherman makes mistakes or misjudges. You have, occasionally, heard him say, "It will rain on Monday", but the rain misses the area, or comes a day later.

This is normal because man can only "guess" the future happening of any event, he cannot confidently predict what will happen with any degree of precision or perfection.

Most traders base their opinions on the fundamentals at the present time and they are unable to see what the fundamentals might be several weeks or months later. But all commodity markets go UP or DOWN in relation to what the "news" will be—in the future.

No man is able enough nor does he have enough time to sit down and try to determine the feelings of many traders towards the market by analyzing the news in this way.

"A company with a large commercial interest in this commodity bought 200 contracts today. Another company with a big commercial interest sold 240 contracts. Another company bought 150 contracts. In addition, 350 speculators bought back their "shorts" and another 250 speculators sold short. Therefore, with that information in front of me, I conclude that the market will definitely move UP."

As he may analyze those buy and sell orders, he may be right on the basic

10

trend. Another man using those same figures may conclude that the market will soon move—DOWN—instead of UP as that first analyst had determined.

To do all of the above analysis in order to determine the true strength or weakness of the market—day after day—for several months would be extremely difficult, time-consuming and very tiring.

No average trader has that much time nor would he have access to all those figures and information so he can make that exhaustive study and evaluation of the market.

But a careful study of the volume and the open interest in a commodity can offer an extra tool to help you gauge the potential power and direction of the market.

The most complete study of the volume and open interest ever written is given in the book—HOW TO BUILD A FORTUNE IN COMMODITIES. (Published by Windsor Books, P. O. Box 280, Brightwaters, N. Y. 11718)

The "moving averages" (as I have worked them out) can save you a tremendous amount of time, effort and confusion because the moving averages digest and analyze the important supply and demand factors for you.

They will also help to give you a more accurate opinion—after a few minutes study—of the true strength or weakness of the market and the direction the market will move—in the future.

This means you can estimate those supply and demand factors more easily so that, in the future, when those supply and demand factors are known, you will find that you have entered your trade so that you will have greater assurance that you will be right with the trend.

To be a winner in commodities, you must learn patience. The fundamentals, in time, will turn from bearish to bullish and then, when a top is reached, they will slowly turn from bullish to bearish once again.

When the market begins to move in your direction, you must hold, wait and try to get the largest profit possible from every move—UP or DOWN.

You must control your emotions and not be content with small profits. That is why very few traders who trade every little move UP and DOWN ever wind up as winners at the end of the year.

The truth is—most of them, when they try to "guess", lose most or all of their money. It is just a question of time how long it will take.

That is one of the reasons why Rule 27 in the book—HOW TO BUILD A FORTUNE IN COMMODITIES—is so important.

Only a professional learns. The amateur never does. And there are many more amateurs trading in commodities than professionals.

This is an age of specialization and "specialists" seem to earn more money than those who are not so carefully trained. Not many individuals are able to tune up their automobile, draw up plans for a house, fix the plumbing in their bathroom or fill their own teeth.

Too much could go wrong. The end result might then be costly.

The logical and sensible thing to do is to seek advice and help from a professional or an advisor who happens to be a "specialist" rather than one who deals or trades in all commodities because, like a "jack of all trades", he will know only a little about each one.

Full-time specialists in commodities, for example, can usually do a better job of analyzing and trading than those who devote only a few hours each day to whatever they may be doing.

In spite of that fact, many traders in commodities still prefer to "do it themselves". They feel that, no matter how many mistakes they make, they are reluctant to pay for professional help and advice. And, worst of all, too many look for and hope to get some sort of tip or advice—"free".

Most brokers provide such advice in a general sort of way. But the record shows that advice given by brokers will, oftentime, cause people to buy near the top of a move (where they should, instead, be selling or looking for a point to sell). Or, they will advise them to sell near the bottom (where they should, instead, be buying or looking for a point to buy).

And that, you may be certain is true of brokers—everywhere—no matter what brokerage firm they may work for.

The reason is—brokers are too busy during the day to analyze the news, keep up their charts, answer the phone many times each day and write up orders to give helpful advice to all those customers who ask for it.

Their job, as brokers, is to fill orders and try to stimulate business from new and old customers. This does not allow them enough time in a four to five hour day to, also, be competent analysts and advisors.

That haphazard reliance on advice from brokers is one of the reasons why the record shows that, over the past 50 years or more, 90% of the people who trade in commodities still lose money.

Most professional traders claim that, if you lose on 50% of your trades (and you make certain your losses are small), you can still earn a large amount of profit every year—provided you have larger profits on the other 50% of your trades.

Obviously, this more professional way to build equity in your account, makes sense. And, if you really want to be one of those 10% who, generally, win, you will need to know a better and more dependable way to earn those profits.

That is the reason for this book. It is a PROFESSIONAL TRADING SYSTEM. And it is one of the tools now being used by three of the world's largest commodity charting services.

2

A PLAN FOR LARGER PROFITS

If you want to earn large profits from commodities, there is only one way—and that is—you must make certain you have a good position—either "long" or "short"—then hold that position for a definite move of two weeks or more—either UP or DOWN.
THERE IS NO OTHER WAY.

Any other system of trading in the past has resulted in a large amount of losses that could have been prevented by taking the emotion, the "hope" and the "guessing" out of your trading.

Everything in life depends on cycles. The four seasons, life and death and the general movement of commodities as they move from oversupply to a comparative shortage of supply. Within those cycles, there are temporary trends that you can use to take some profits from long positions or buy back your "shorts" or "hedged" positions.

Almost every trader who has the wisdom to look for "special situations" to develop and has the patience to wait for those opportunities to develop on their charts can, eventually, build a fortune in commodities.

While that is true, what actually happens is, soon after you decide to be a wise and prudent trader, you may begin to think (as so many eventual losers do), "Now I am really smart. Now I can really make that million."

When those thoughts come into your mind, you forget the wise, patient and conservative rules you need to follow to earn that large amount of money.

With such thoughts, you will fall, once again, into the same pattern of mistakes that cause 90% of the traders to lose.

Then, you will no longer be one of the 10% who win.

THE MISTAKES MOST TRADERS MAKE

Many thousands of men and women who trade in commodities "hope" to make a lot of money. Many of them, however, take a position on impulse rather than on some understanding of the way the market will trend. Then they wait to get "lucky".

That is not speculation in the true sense of the word. That is gambling. And nobody who "gambles" in commodities will ever be a winner for long.

Jesse Livermore, the legendary speculator who made millions of dollars trading in commodities, but wound up losing most of his capital said, "It would have been wiser, on my part, if I had traded less often and searched for a larger percentage of profit over a period of time. My income, therefore, would have been much larger."

Such traders as Jesse Livermore fail to earn as much money as they would like to earn because they continue to make the same mistakes several times. And, too often, they break one or more of the important—27 Rules—given in Chapter 10 of the book—HOW TO BUILD A FORTUNE IN COMMODITIES—(Windsor Books, P. O. Box 280, Brightwaters, N. Y. 11718).

Mistakes in commodities, however, are never fatal—especially if you always remember to get out of a losing position before you take a larger loss.

> If you should take a loss, stand aside for at least
> two full days. Do not trade. Somehow your analysis
> of the market was not right at that time.

Or you may find that, if you are not trading and you look at your charts, some other commodity may offer a better opportunity than the one you had been watching so closely.

Look at the action of that market more closely on your charts. You will find that, after a few more days of trading, the movement of prices on your charts (especially the closing prices), will give you a much clearer picture.

Fortunately—there is always another day. Another opportunity will always arise in some commodity a few days after your mistake was made.

All you need is the capital and the courage to take advantage of a new "special situation" when you see it developing on your "moving average" charts.

If you learn from your mistakes, and you should, you will, eventually be a success. But, if you are hard-headed, lose heart or give up, you will never win in the long run or regain whatever you may have lost because—

YOUR LOSS OF CONFIDENCE IS
THE GREATEST LOSS YOU CAN EVER SUFFER

If you should lose some money, or even most of your money through some bad trades, you must remember that, if you look for and trade in "special situations" as described in the book—HOW TO BUILD A FORTUNE IN COMMODITIES—you can recover that loss and, by carefully following this Professional Trading System, you can earn some more.

But, once you lose your confidence, you are unable to reason clearly. You are, then, afraid to buy or sell even though your charts show a potential "special situation" is developing.

In fact, if you select the right commodity, then stay with a definite trend—UP or DOWN—and earn large profits five or six times every year, your profits for the year could run as high as 700% or more. And this book will show you some ways you can do this—especially if you know how to compound your profit.

If that is true—why doesn't everyone earn such a large profit?

First—they don't know how.

Second—they tend to take too many small profits—or—

Third—they trade too often—usually several times every week—hoping to "scalp" the market. But, like Jesse Livermore pointed out, this is definitely not wise.

Fourth—they are too lazy to do the "homework" necessary to earn those large potential profits.

Fifth—they are unwilling to spend the money to buy the right tools so they can know instead of "guess".

Sixth—they prefer, instead, to look for easy ways, "tips" and "free advice" when common sense dictates that tips and free advice are seldom worthwhile.

Seventh—they break one or more of the 27 Rules given in the book—HOW TO BUILD A FORTUNE IN COMMODITIES. And, if one or more of those 27 Rules are broken, there will certainly be losses— instead of profits.

Finally—they are inclined to rely, too often, on advice from their broker. They do not realize their broker does not have the time nor the know-how to give professional and continuous advice concerning commodities.

The broker's job is to enter orders to buy or sell— it is not to give advice. His time, therefore, is limited. And my long experience as an internationally-known Commodity Advisor proves that—the advisory business is a full-time job that requires a great deal of experience, time and energy determining the many different factors that can influence a change in price and trend.

That is why a broker cannot be an advisor. And an advisor does not have the time nor the facilities to be an efficient broker.

Because the above facts are true, this book was written to overcome those problems. If you do overcome those problems, you can earn a

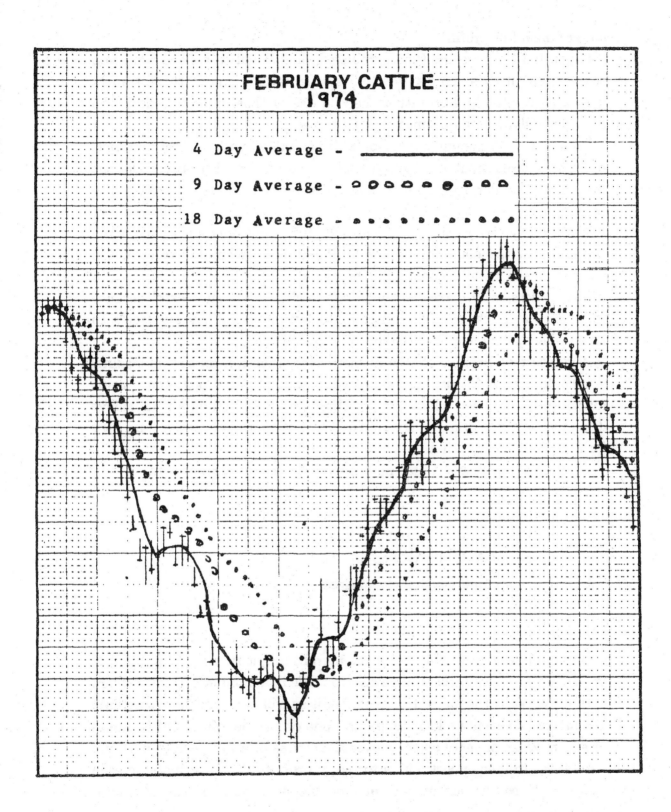

FEBRUARY CATTLE
1974

4 Day Average -

9 Day Average -

18 Day Average -

19

larger amount of profit.

If you fail to overcome those problems, or you fail to believe what you see written on these pages, you will surely become one of those traders who will, eventually, lose rather than be one of those better traders who can, generally, win more times than they lose.

As a former Commodity Advisor who has talked with several hundreds of traders throughout the United States, Canada and Europe, I find the majority of traders continue to make one or more of the mistakes outlined above.

A few really serious traders eventually learn, but only a few. Too many traders want to "get rich overnight". They never seem to overcome the desire to make a lot of money—in a hurry.

The traders, who make money in commodities, are successful because they seem to know which commodity to buy or sell. They also seem to know when to buy or sell at the most favorable times.

If you earn an average of 30% or more every month from careful trading, you could earn 300% or more every year. And, if you repeat those gains for several years, you will be one of those successful traders who believe it is much wiser to win and try for that 30% or more per month than "try for a million" and lose it all.

To do this, you must—first—determine whether the market is in—

1—a definite UP trend
2—a definite DOWN trend—or—
3—an indecisive, **trading market**

Once you determine which way the market might move—UP or DOWN or SIDEWAYS—you will then be able to trade in a more intelligent manner.

In most years, the majority of commodities will have one or two definite UP moves of seven weeks or more and one or two definite DOWN moves of seven weeks or more so that, over the course of a full year, you should have three to four opportunities for large profits—(100% or more on each of those three to four moves—in any one of several of the 20 major commodities).

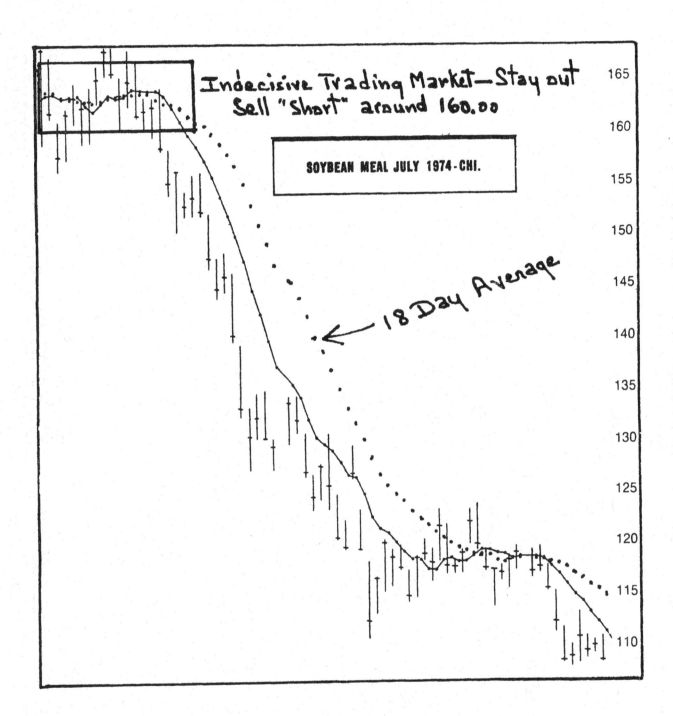

Indecisive Trading Market—Stay out
Sell "Short" around 160.00

SOYBEAN MEAL JULY 1974-CHI.

18 Day Average

3

THE IMPORTANCE
OF MOVING AVERAGES

The "moving averages", as I have developed them, will help you earn larger profits in both bull markets and bear markets. They take into consideration the two most important elements necessary for profitable trades— TIME and PRICE CHANGE.

The moving averages can help you earn those larger profits for six reasons.

1. By looking at your moving average figures every day together with your bar charts, you will be able to gauge, more accurately, when the trend of the market may turn definitely and persistently from UP to DOWN—or—from DOWN to UP.

2. The moving averages help you eliminate the wrong opinions, rumors and the news that create so much confusion and cause so many traders to lose money including some of the traders on the floor of the exchange—if they rely, too often, on the wrong opinions, rumor and news.

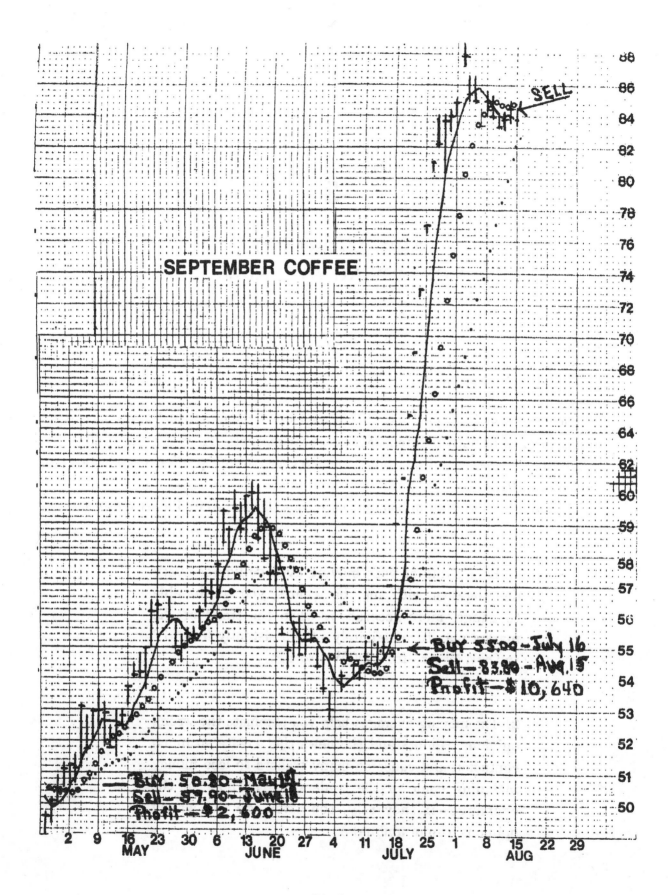

SEPTEMBER COFFEE

SELL

←Buy-55.00-July 16
Sell-83.80-Aug. 15
Profit-$10,640

Buy-50.80-May 9
Sell-57.90-June 6
Profit-$2,600

MAY   JUNE   JULY   AUG

24

3. During indecisive, "trading markets," the price movement patterns you see on a bar chart can, oftentimes, be deceptive and costly. But the traders who use the moving averages are able to be more patient. They also find it is easier to buy and sell with more confidence—especially if they read and mind the words in large letters on pages 55 and 56.

4. A careful compilation of the moving averages each day will help you see, more clearly, why the trend is definitely going to change. And it will make that change in trend without you having to analyze the news in order to reach a judgment.

5. Once the moving averages have pointed out that change in trend, the market will move strongly and definitely in the direction of that change—either UP or DOWN. It will continue to move persistently in spite of the news which is slowly changing to agree with the trend.

6. As soon as the moving averages convince you, by their persistence, that the trend will continue to move in your favor for several days to several weeks—you can then pyramid (buy or sell more contracts) and, thereby, gain some additional profits—if the market continues to move in that direction.

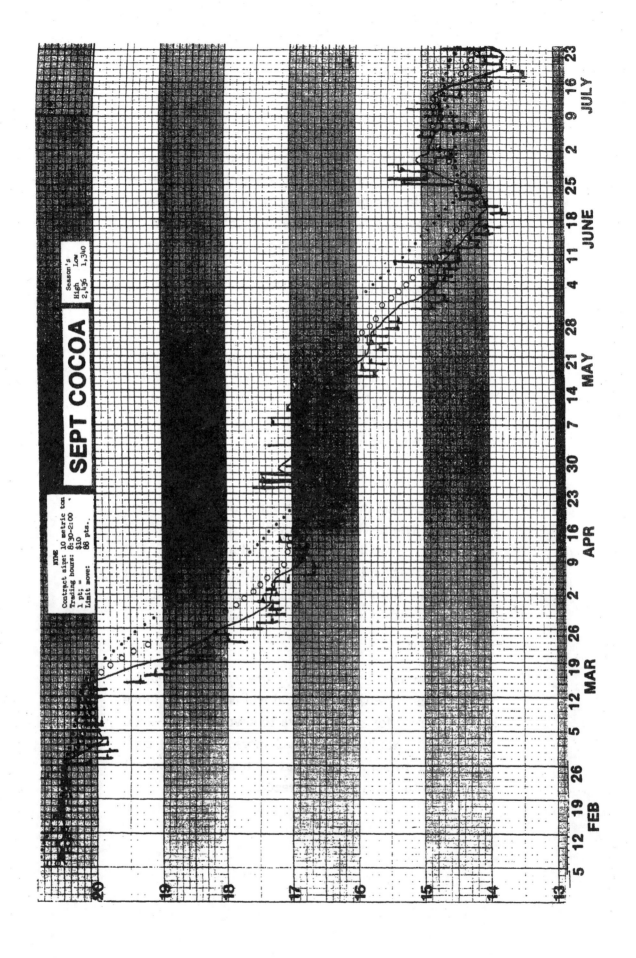

4

HOW TO COMPILE
THE MOVING AVERAGES

To compile the moving averages, you need to buy a dozen or more sheets of 5×10 chart paper (size 11″×17″) from any good office supply or art store. You will need one sheet for every commodity you plan to trade.

Note—any chart paper smaller than 11″×17″ will not give you enough accuracy—and accuracy is always important if you want to earn large profits from commodities.

For a starting date, select a Friday and mark that date at the bottom of your chart paper. Then count forward five more squares and mark it for the next Friday. Continue counting five squares and enter Friday dates for several weeks in advance. The price range should be marked at the left hand side of your paper in the same way that you mark the prices on your bar charts.

To compile the 9 day moving average, select one monthly contract of the commodity you prefer to trade. Add the closing prices for the 9 days previous to that first Friday. Then, divide the total of those 9 closing days by 9 to get the first point for your 9 day moving average.

On the tenth day, add the closing price for that tenth day to the total for the previous 9 days. This will give you a new total. Then, subtract the first closing figure of the previous 9 days. Divide this new total by 9 and enter that figure above the Monday line on your chart paper.

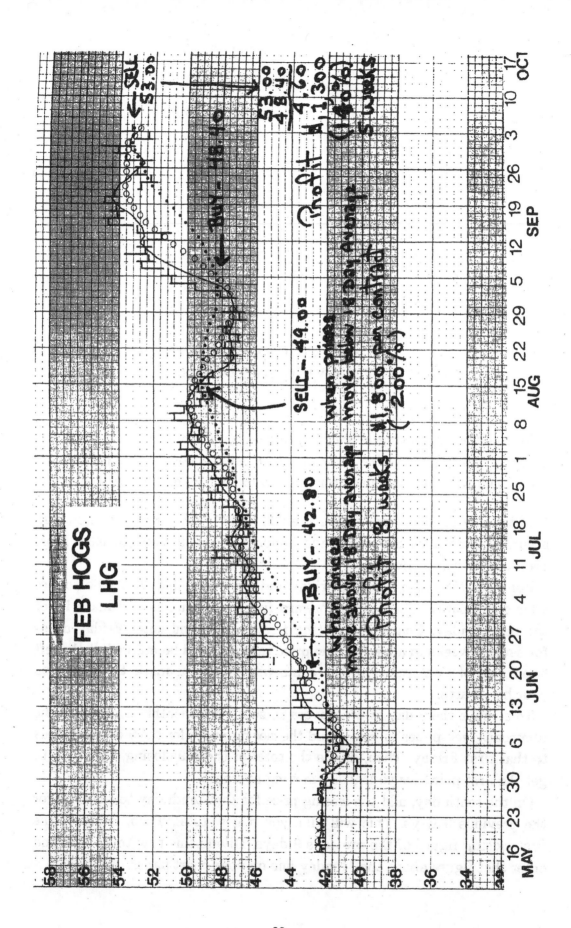

FEB HOGS.
LHG

←SELL
53.00

←BUY – 48.40

SELL – 49.00

When prices
move below 18 Day Average

53.00
48.40
4.60

Profit $1,300

(14.0%)
5 weeks

$1,800 per contract

(200%)

←BUY – 42.80

When prices
move above 18 Day Average

Profit $1,800 8 weeks

On the eleventh day, repeat the procedure used for the tenth day. Continue adding and subtracting the same way, every day, until 30 days before that contract goes off the board. At that time, follow the same procedure with the next nearest contract.

The 4 day average and the 18 day average are compiled in the same way as the plotting of the 9 day average as described above.

Note—The reason the high and the low prices of the day are not used is because experience has proved that the closing price is the only price of real importance because, during each day, floor traders, other speculators and scalpers who try to day trade make up their minds just before the close whether they will take a position overnight and at what price most of them will be satisfied to hold their overnight position. This tends to give a more realistic price to the closing of the market.

Prices may fluctuate wildly as opinions and judgments are made, but the closing price will be a more accurate guide.

Most successful traders do not take a position in a market solely on "hope" or in an opinion based upon "guess" that the market will "break out" in a definite direction—UP or DOWN. Instead they prefer to wait and let the market give them a "signal" to either BUY or SELL.

In simple words—they miss buying near the bottom and also miss selling near the top. But, when the breakout does come, they can go with the trend of the market UP or DOWN and make a large amount of profit between that breakout just above the base near the bottom or sell just before the market completes its top and gets ready to move sharply lower once again.

To make this point more clear—you can safely buy at Point A—on the following chart—and sell at Point B. The difference in price is 70 cents. Your total net profit in that Wheat trade would be $3,440 per contract. Your profit on 2 contracts would be $6,880. And, on 10 contracts, your profit would be $34,400.

And, if you sold "short" at Point B, you would have an opportunity for another large profit as prices decline once again.

Note very carefully that those large profits are possible in spite of the fact that you missed a large portion of the bottom of the bullish move (UP)

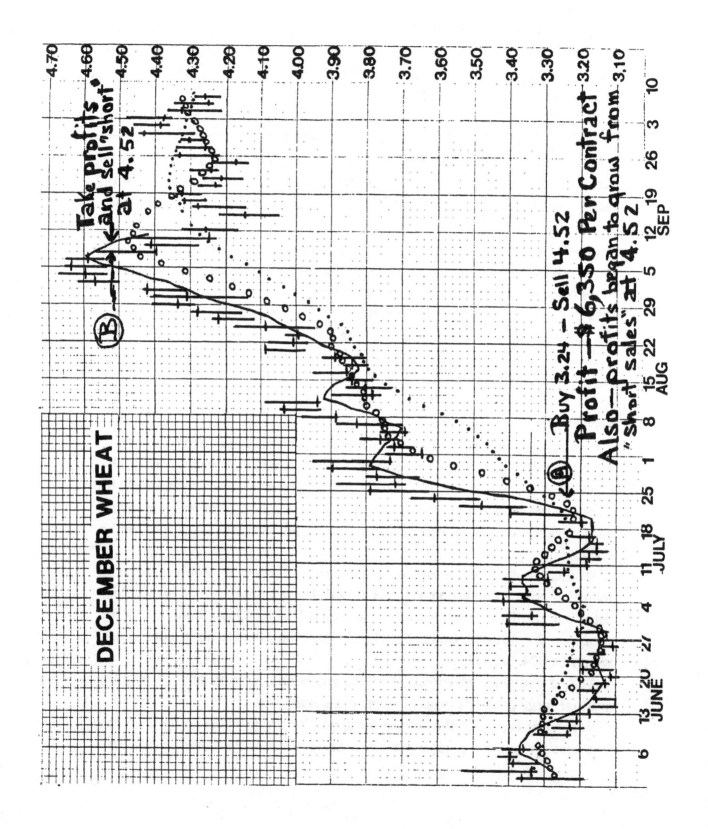

DECEMBER WHEAT

Take Profits "and sell"short" at 4.52

Sell 4.52
Buy 3.24 —
Profit — $6,350 Per Contract
Also—profits began to grow from 3.10
"Short" sales" at 4.52

30

and a large portion of the top before the bear move (DOWN) began at Point B.

By understanding this failure to buy at the bottom and sell near the top, you will eliminate two of the biggest "mental hangups"most traders have and that is—(1) they want to get off a "perfect trade" and (2) it will help them to be able to understand, more clearly, how to "gear up their minds" to buy and go long when a "bull market" begins to gain a definite and persistent upside momentum and, also how to "gear up their minds" to sell "short" before the "bear market" begins a definite and persistent downside momentum.

As you can see, it requires a great deal of painstaking time every day to compile those three moving averages and place them on your charts. But the extra profits you can earn from that effort can be larger with those charts in front of you than they would be without them so you will find it worthwhile to devote several hours of your time each trading day to keep those charts up to date.

If your time is limited, you will find it wise to pay someone else a few dollars each week to do that work for you. I suggest, therefore, that you subscribe to a chart service that features the moving averages as I have developed them.

Because my time is also limited, I find it is best for me to pay a reliable company for all the time, effort and expense for doing this—especially when the fee they charge is tax deductible.

The name and address of the chart service I personally use is—

COMMODITY TREND SERVICE, INC.
1224 U.S. Hwy 1 - Cove Plaza
North Palm Beach Fl 33408

I can recommend this chart service very highly. Their charts are large, easy to read and they place the moving averages directly over the daily prices.

This is more helpful because you can quickly see, at a glance, how the movement of each commodity is progressing so you can, more accurately, see when the moving averages will indicate a definite change in trend.

You can get a sample copy of a complete set of charts from the above company. All you need to do is—send your name and address to them at the address above and ask for a FREE sample copy.

As of July, 1982 two other chart services give the R. C. Allen 4, 9 and 18 day averages. They are—

COMMODITY   COMMODITY PRICE
PERSPECTIVE   CHARTS
327 South LaSalle St.   219 Parkade
Chicago, Ill. 60604   Cedar Falls, Iowa 50613

, A sample copy of the above two chart services will be sent for $10. But the moving averages are placed in a small box at the side of the daily price charts. This makes it a bit more difficult to determine the exact breakout point. But this added service is still better than not using the 4, 9 and 18 day averages at all.

5

THE SIX MISTAKES
MOST UNSUCCESSFUL TRADERS MAKE

1. They spend too much time around brokerage offices. They forget that—no "rich traders" can be found in any brokerage office.

2. They listen, too often, to the view of their brokers. But brokers do not have the time to study, analyze and advise clients. That is why brokers are, so often, wrong in their viewpoints. (A broker's job is, simply, to enter orders to buy and sell and make certain those orders are filled at the right time and price.)

3. They read and study the "news" and they are lulled into believing the "bullish news" will continue and prices will remain at a high level—or—the "bearish news" will continue and prices will remain at a low level.

As a general rule, you can sell the market—just before prices decline. And a lot of "bearish news" is generally prevalent near the bottom of a move—just before prices begin to rise once again.

This is, generally true, also of stocks and bonds as well as commodities.

33

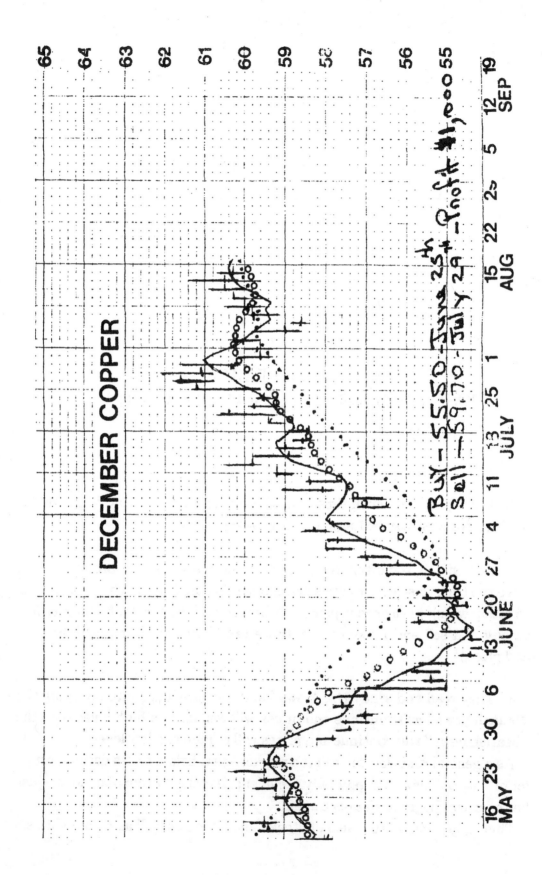

DECEMBER COPPER

Buy – 55.50 – June 25th
Sell – 59.70 – July 29 – Profit #1,000

65
64
63
62
61
60
59
58
57
56
55

16 23 30 6 13 20 27 4 11 13 25 1 15 22 29 5 12 19
MAY   JUNE   JULY   AUG   SEP

34

4. They are inclined to look for and take small profits.

5. They get out of a good position too soon—just as a good move in one direction is about to begin. This limits their profits and violates the rule— When the market begins to move in your favor, let your profits build so that your net gains will be large enough each month to offset any small losses you may have to take.

6. They refuse to take small losses—if they are wrong. Or—they refuse to get out of a losing position and hold on too long—if the market continues to move against them.

Too often, in such cases, this causes them to lose all or most of their capital.

It will be wise to analyze your mistakes. If you should lose money on a trade—and you will—because EVERYONE MAKES MISTAKES—(including the best of professionals)—analyze the mistake you made and learn from it.

Reading this book over and over again—many times—will help you because —on one page or another—you will find the answer.

IN EVERY COMMODITY MARKET
THERE ARE FOUR GENERAL AREAS OF CONGESTION

1. Final tops – before the start of a new "bear market".

2. Areas of distribution as prices move lower. (See A – B – C – below)

3. Final bottoms – before the start of a new "bull market".

4. Areas of accumulation as prices move higher. (See D – E – F – below)

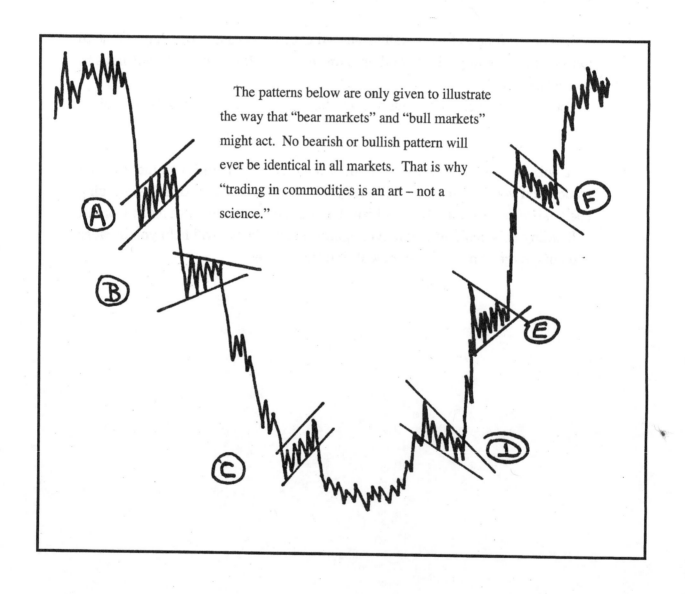

The patterns below are only given to illustrate the way that "bear markets" and "bull markets" might act. No bearish or bullish pattern will ever be identical in all markets. That is why "trading in commodities is an art – not a science."

6

HOW TO IMPROVE YOUR "LUCK"

Most successful traders admit they make mistakes. And some traders are wrong as many times as they are right because—neither people nor the markets are perfect.

But traders, who are successful, make certain they follow one important rule—"If you are wrong—take a small loss quickly and get out of that trade."

If you are out of the market or you wait a few more trading days, you will be able to look at your "moving averages" chart and get a fresh viewpoint. Then you can decide to trade again in a way that will help you to go with the potential trend.

If you are right and the trend begins to move in your favor, let your profits build so that your net gains will be large enough each month to offset any small losses you may have to take. The "moving averages" will help you gain that extra profit.

Considering all of the information, trading tools and chart services that are available today, there should no longer be such a thing as a "naive" investor in commodities. Every individual who decides to invest money— whether it is in stocks, bonds, real estate or commodities, can find some one person or group with more than average knowledge and, possibly, some expert foresight.

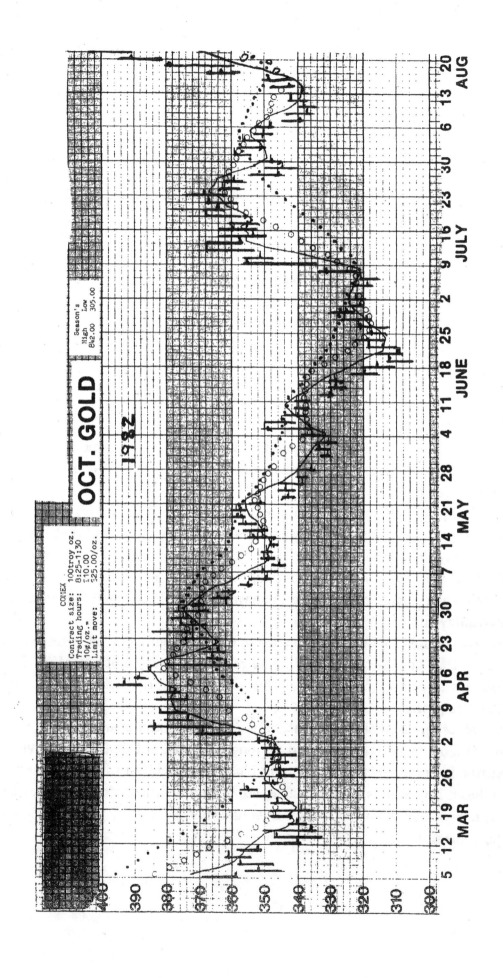

The truth is—if such a naive individual invests his money blindly, without some sort of experienced help or without the guidance of a book like this, he is not an investor at all. He is just one of those unfortunate individuals who will, eventually, lose.

That is why you must learn all that you can and, especially, make every effort to trade like a professional.

Your "luck" will improve when you have the knowledge and the know-how to take advantage of an opportunity when it comes.

If you look over the charts that contain my 4, 9 and 18 day "moving averages" for the 20 major commodities, you will find that one or more "special situations" will occur almost every month.

That means that if you carefully watch all of those 20 major commodities, you could find as many as 8 to 10 very profitable "special situations" every year.

These "special situations" offer you better opportunities for profit than you will find in some of the other commodities where, from time to time, the picture is not quite as clear.

And it is most important for you to feel that the potential for profit on each "special situation" you see is, at least three times larger than your potential loss if you should happen to be wrong in your judgment.

Fear and greed cause the largest losses for the majority of traders because— under the influence of fear and greed, they are inclined to trade without careful thought and reason.

Fear, for example, causes traders to take large losses because they "fear" they might lose more. That is why markets will, so often, turn around and move in the opposite direction when all those who are "afraid" are forced out of their positions.

Greed causes traders to "overtrade". They buy or sell too many contracts in an effort to "make a lot of money in a hurry." Or, they jump in and out of a market when logic or reason says—"be conservative."

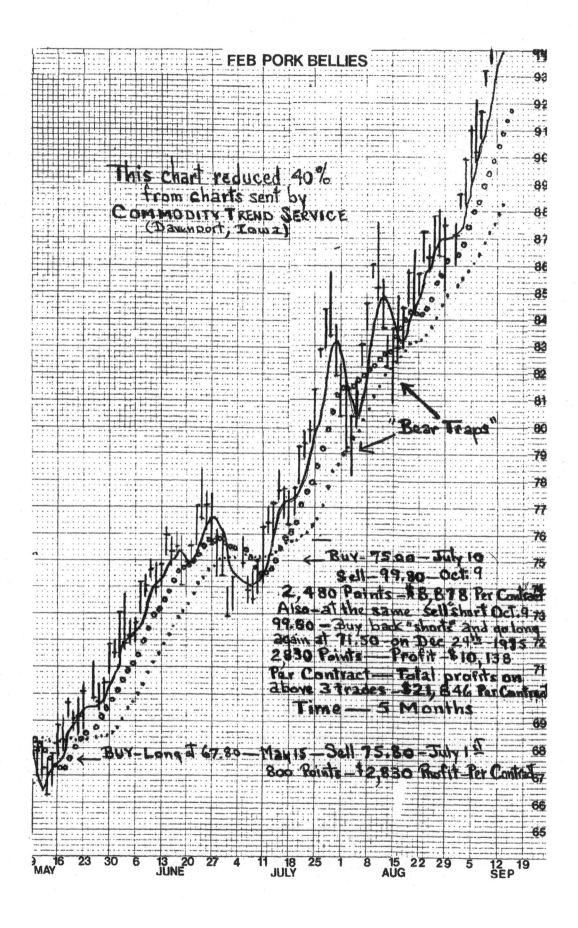

FEB PORK BELLIES

This chart reduced 40%
from charts sent by
COMMODITY TREND SERVICE
(Davenport, Iowa)

"Bear Traps"

← Buy - 75.00 - July 10
Sell - 99.80 - Oct. 9
2,480 Points - $8,878 Per Contract
Also - at the same Sell short Oct. 9
99.80 - Buy back "shorts" and go long
again at 71.50 on Dec 24th 1975
2830 Points - Profit - $10,138
Per Contract - Total profits on
above 3 trades $21,846 Per Contract
Time — 5 Months

← BUY - Long # 67.80 - May 15 - Sell 75.80 - July 1
800 Points - $2,830 Profit Per Contract

This book, therefore is designed for the more serious traders who want to know—HOW TO WIN—and are willing to look for the "special situations" that can create the large profits that come from following a definite trend—UP or DOWN for a period of ten days or more.

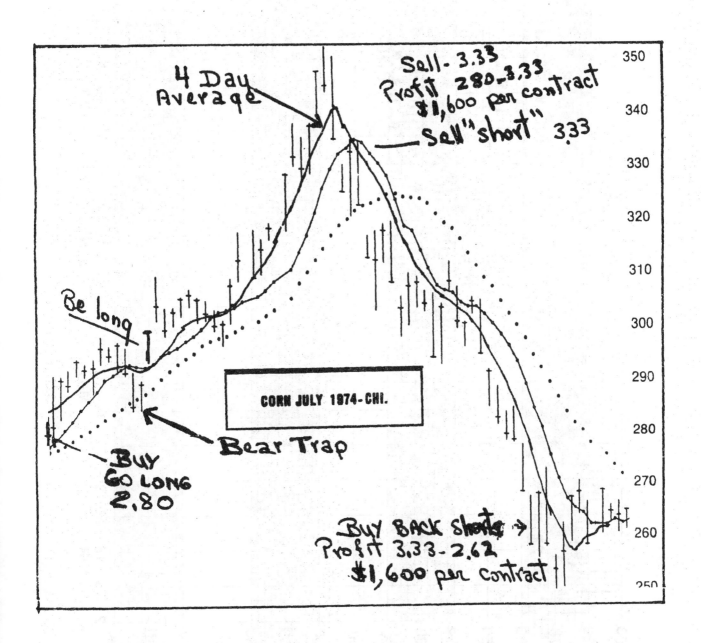

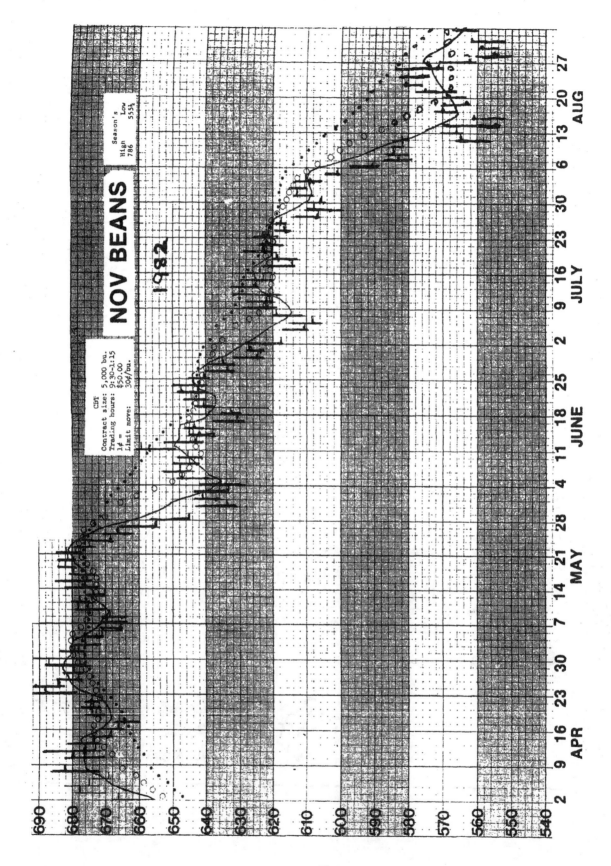

NOV BEANS

1982

CBT
Contract size: 5,000 bu.
Trading hours: 9:30-1:15
1¢ = $50.00
Limit move: 30¢/bu.

Season's
High   Low
786   555½

42

7

DON'T TAKE QUICK PROFITS
INSTEAD—LET YOUR PROFITS GROW

42 years of experience as a trader and commodity advisor has proved there is nothing more sad than to watch the many individuals who walk into a brokerage office early in the morning or call their broker and say, "What looks like a good trade today?"

They "hope", unfortunately for some piece of news or information that can help them make some money that particular day.

In brief, those individuals are not interested in large profits. They seem to get no pleasure out of earning $2,000—$3,000—$4,000 or more profit per contract. They prefer, instead, to "gamble", "take a chance" or "hope" that, during that particular day, they will gain a net profit of $100 to $200.

Occasionally, of course, they do gain such profits. But, on other days, they cannot get out of their position fast enough. Then, they lose several hundred dollars or more.

At the end of the month, they have helped their broker earn a large amount of money in commissions, but their equity may show only a small gain—or a loss.

As a general rule, when traders "hope" for quick profits, instead of long-term profits, they eventually lose all of their capital. Too often, they lack the patience necessary to hold a position through a period of consolidation and take advantage of the definite move—UP or DOWN—after the "break out" occurs.

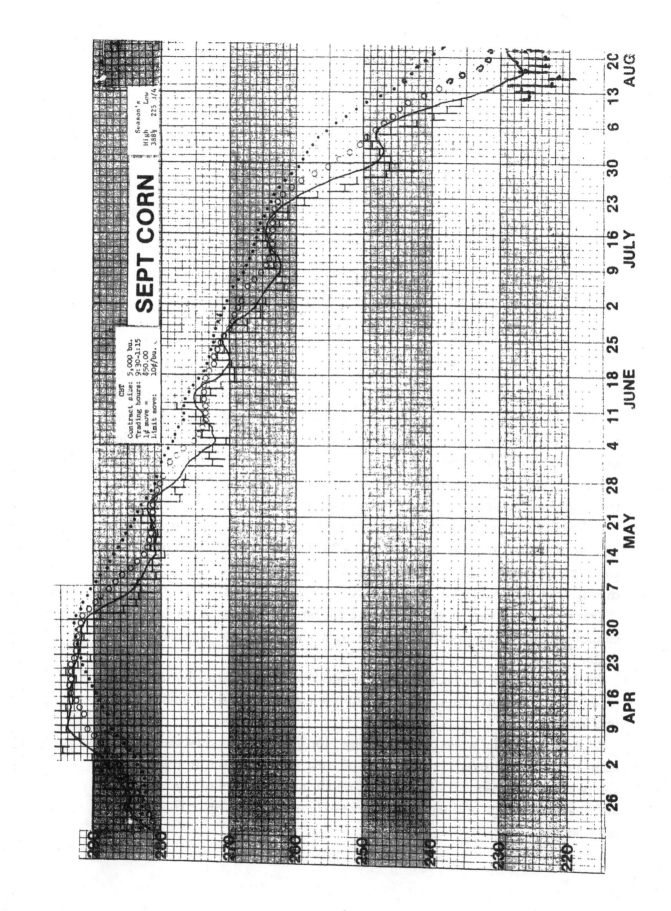

SEPT CORN

CBT
Contract size: 5,000 bu.
Trading hours: 9:30-1:15
1¢ move = $50.00
limit move: 10¢/bu.

Season's
High 388½
Low 225 J/4

44

8

NEVER TRY TO GET
THE PERFECT TRADE

Too many traders look for "the perfect trade" and, if they miss buying near the bottom or miss selling near the top, they are inclined not to enter the market. Instead, they seem to be content with saying, "I missed the move. I should have done it—yesterday—or last week"—as the case may be.

This is an unfortunate frame of mind because—if a trend is going to continue moving—UP or DOWN—for two weeks or more, you can always get into that market and take a large profit from a trade so long as you let the "moving averages" guide you and you trade with the trend, according to the indication given by the "moving averages" as this book points out.

For example—a very successful trader once told me—"I made my fortune because I never tried to buy at the bottom nor sell at the top. I was satisfied to buy when values were, generally, high—without regards to final tops or final bottoms—which no one can know or identify until after they have been definitely made. And, except by some lucky "guesses", they are impossible to ascertain."

When prices are high and a "top" seems to be indicated, you can only earn large profits by selling "short". But the majority of traders, at that time, are reluctant to "sell short".

They hear or read "bullish news". As this bullish news becomes more widely known, they are, then inclined to buy—even though prices are high in relation to prices several weeks ago.

Many of those same traders who were so reluctant to buy because they "missed the bottom" are now more willing to buy—even though prices are high in relation to prices several weeks ago.

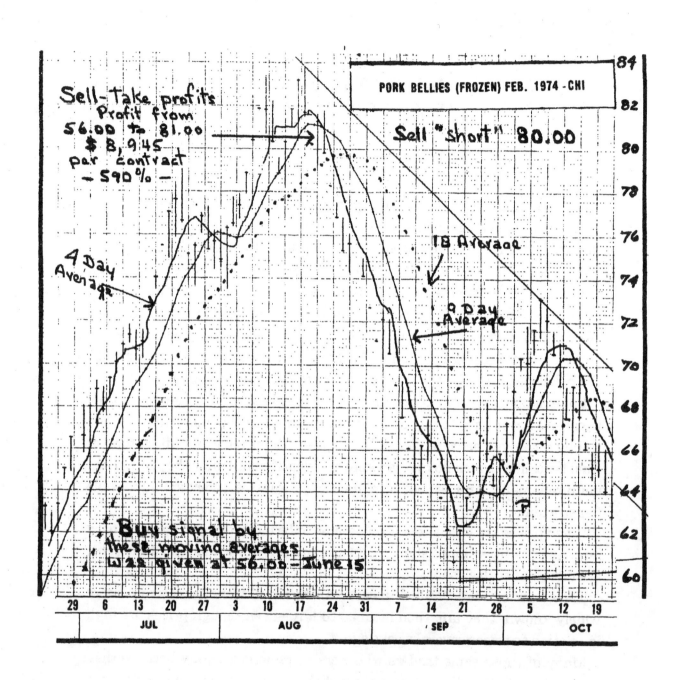

Sell-take profits
Profit from
56.00 to 81.00
$ 8,945
per contract
— 590% —

PORK BELLIES (FROZEN) FEB. 1974 - CHI

Sell "short" 80.00

4 Day
Average

18 Average

9 Day
Average

Buy signal by
these moving averages
was given at 56.00 - June 15

| 29 | 6 | 13 | 20 | 27 | 3 | 10 | 17 | 24 | 31 | 7 | 14 | 21 | 28 | 5 | 12 | 19 |

JUL   AUG   SEP   OCT

46

Many of those same traders who were so reluctant to buy because they missed the bottom are now more willing to buy because the bullish news they hear gives them confidence that the market will continue strong and move a bit higher.

They do not realize that all of the knowledgeable traders—especially those with a large commercial interest in that market, are taking profits or putting in hedges for protection against a move towards lower prices.

They begin to sell before the next major move begins which those commercial traders believe will be DOWN.

When prices decline—instead of rise—as they had "hoped for"—that same majority of traders seem to prefer to hold on. They will only sell when prices have fallen a considerable way, have made new lows, or they hear an increased amount of "bearish news."

This desire to buy near the top and sell near the bottom is the reason why 90% of the traders have always lost money. And this tendency, unfortunately, seems to be true of all investors. It makes no difference whether their investments are in stocks, bonds or commodities.

Now you can see why—if you are one of those 10% of traders who, generally, win—you can earn large profits from those 90% who, generally, lose.

As an example of why it is wise to wait for the right "special situation" and take large profits out of the market, I would like to give you the following true story.

Between August 9th and August 17th, 1973, I sold 30 contracts of February (1974) Pork Bellies "short" between 78.00 and 82.50.

Those sales were premature. And they were sold short in spite of the very bullish news that was being issued at that time.

Several brokerage houses were predicting that Pork Bellies would soon reach 90 cents. If they reached that level, I would have been completely "wiped out" with a tremendous loss on those 30 contracts.

But, as I pointed out above, I was willing to remain "short" because I knew that the fundamentals, in the near future, would become a bit more "bearish" and prices would, therefore, justify a decline.

The market topped out at 83.80, broke sharply, then declined for several weeks. After prices closed below the prices at which I had sold those 30 contracts, my profits began to increase at a rapid rate.

The 18 day average now was the guide for the downside movement so I sold more contracts "short" every time that prices had a small rally during each of the days the moving averages indicated that prices would continue to move lower.

Soon I was "short" the legal limit of 250 contracts. On the day that Bellies made their first bottom, the market opened "limit down". I bought back all 250 contracts with a net profit of over $700,000.

While I was making that large profit, the customers who traded with brokers who predicted that bellies would reach 90 cents, lost a tremendous amount of money.

Obviously, when you can be "right with the trend"—UP or DOWN—you can earn much larger profits than you can by trying to take quick profits several times each week.

But—how can you determine that trend—UP or DOWN—and stay with that trend so those large profits can be earned.

That is the purpose of this book. To show you—not the perfect way, but a comparatively safe way that, in the majority of cases, will help you earn several thousands of dollars in extra profits—every year.

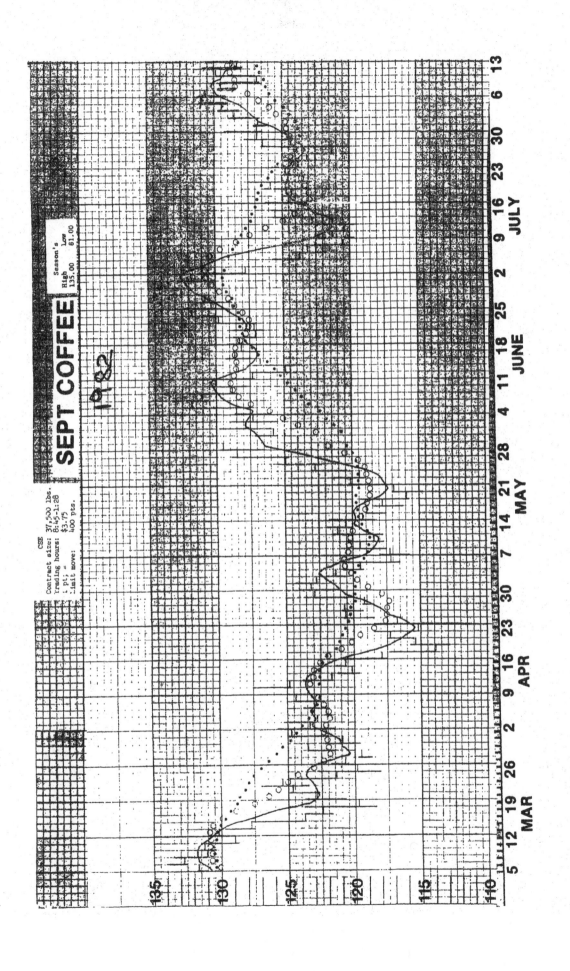

9

WHEN TO BUY
FOR LARGER PROFITS

When you compile the moving averages or receive a weekly commodity chart service from one of the charting services that contains a clear and easy to read set of charts of the moving averages, you must look for "the signal" that will suggest you BUY close to the bottom of a "bull move".

This signal will give you a good indication of approximately what day the trend will change from DOWN to UP.

You can estimate what day that change in trend might be by watching the 4 day average and the 9 day average very closely.

When you see that prices for the commodity you are watching will move up and close at a price near or slightly above the 4 day average—buy back all of your "short" positions and go lightly long.

In other words, when you want to establish new long positions, use only ⅓ of the equity in your account.

At that day, the 9 day average should be moving down so that it will cross or touch the 4 day average. This indicates that the "bearish" momentum of the past two weeks or months is slowing down.

But remember that—if prices continue to sell below the 18 day average, you CANNOT go "safely long" or be heavily committed in that market. The reason is—

A MAJOR, SUSTAINED AND PROFITABLE
MOVE UP CANNOT OCCUR UNTIL PRICES
CLOSE ABOVE THE 18 DAY AVERAGE

51

As soon as prices move to a point where they will definitely close at a price above the 4 day and the 9 day averages, you can then use another ⅓ of your capital and add to your long positions.

Finally—before the close of the day that prices move up to or near the point where they will definitely be above the 18 day average, buy some additional contracts for the "breakout move" that, in most commodities, will then begin to pick up speed as prices move higher.

You now have a very nice profit on the original contracts you bought near the bottom—a good profit on the second group of contracts and a good potential for profit on the last group of contracts you bought when prices definitely moved above the 18 day average.

Note—While the above plan will give you very large profits on a comparatively safe basis, it will not assure you of large profits every time you use that rule.

Why?

Because—NO RULE in commodities is perfect. If there were a perfect rule, everyone would soon know it. Then the profits would be very small because you can only earn large profits in commodities from the majority of people who happen to be wrong.

Occasionally, "traps" will occur and you must not, at that time, allow your emotions to cause you to fall into that trap. One more trading day, and especially the closing price of that one more trading day, will put the market, once again into a more realistic and honest trading pattern.

While "traps" do not occur very often, you must continually be on the watch for them—in case the market fails to follow through for any reason whatsoever.

Traps will be discussed further in this book. And many of the charts will show you how these traps look. Notice the closing price on the day the trap occurs. And what occurs after the trap is completed. And learn how you can protect yourself—if you should be caught in either a "bull trap" or a "bear trap."

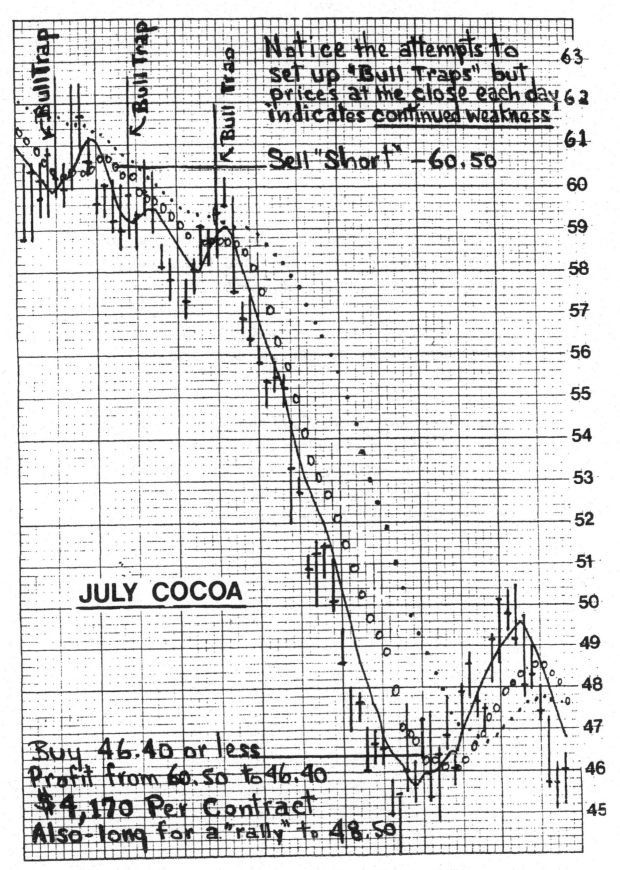

Bull Trap

Bull Trap

Bull Trap

Notice the attempts to
set up "Bull Traps" but
prices at the close each day
indicates continued weakness

Sell "Short" —60.50

JULY COCOA

Buy 46.40 or less
Profit from 60.50 to 46.40
$4,170 Per Contract
Also-long for a "rally" to 48.50

The next two pages can be worth thousands of dollars to you—or—you can save thousands of dollars in losses—if you observe them.

Remember or copy the following two pages. Hang them openly on your wall, at home or in your office.

Over the years, hundreds of thousands of people have lost millions of dollars because they traded, at one time or another, in a way that disregarded these two rules—hoping to "scalp" the market or try to gamble against the trend—UP or DOWN.

When a "bull market" begins

NEVER--NEVER SELL

When prices are trading above the 4 Day, 9 Day and 18 Day MOVING AVERAGES

This means you must be "long" and looking for higher prices and you must never take profits on your "long positions" until a top has been indicated.

REGARDLESS OF NEWS OR FUNDAMENTALS

When a "bear market" begins

NEVER--NEVER BUY

When prices are trading below the 4 Day, 9 Day and 18 Day MOVING AVERAGES

REGARDLESS OF NEWS OR FUNDAMENTALS

This means you must be "short" and looking for lower prices and
you must never take profits on your "short sales" until a bottom has
been indicated.

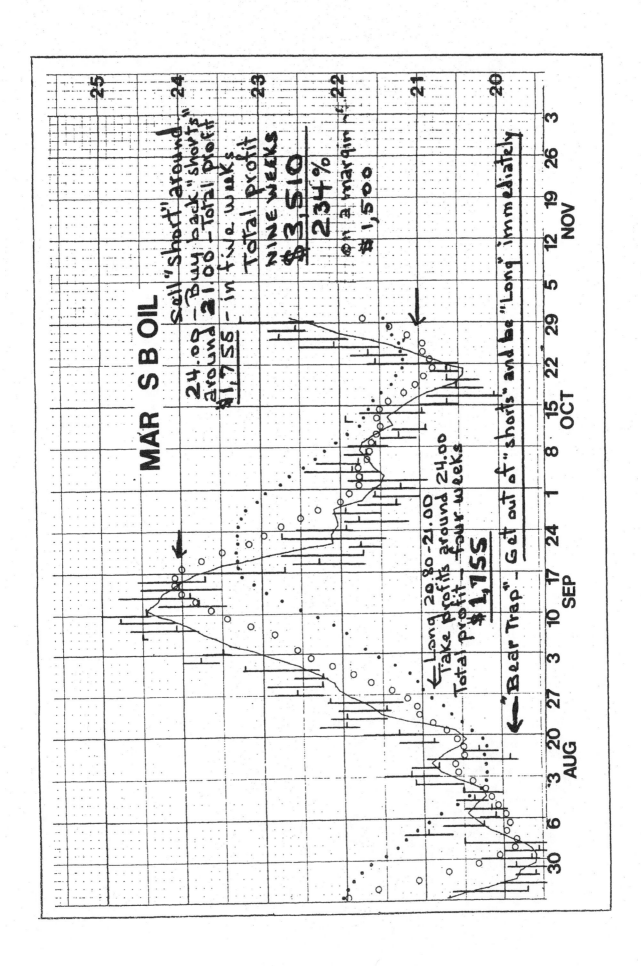

10

WHEN TO SELL
FOR LARGER PROFITS

All commodity markets tend to decline in price faster than they rise in price. The reason is—prices have to be moved up by people who are unwilling to buy at continually higher prices.

But, in a "bear trend" prices can fall fast because all that is needed to create that fast decline is to have a large number of traders step aside and refuse to buy. Also, "weak longs" can easily be influenced by brokers who fear prices will move lower.

You must, therefore, know how and when to take profits on long positions and when to sell "short" on a comparatively safe basis.

The first indication that a possible new, long-term "bear market" is beginning will usually come when prices close at or near the 4 day average.

This is the first signal that the market may be reaching a top. At this time, you must get ready to take your profits on all long positions.

A few days later, if you see the 9 day average is moving up close to the 4 day average or touching the 4 day average, you must then consider selling "short".

You can estimate what day that change in trend from UP to DOWN might occur by watching the 4 day average and the 9 day average very closely. When you see that prices will move down and close at a price near or slightly below the 4 day average, take profits on all your long positions

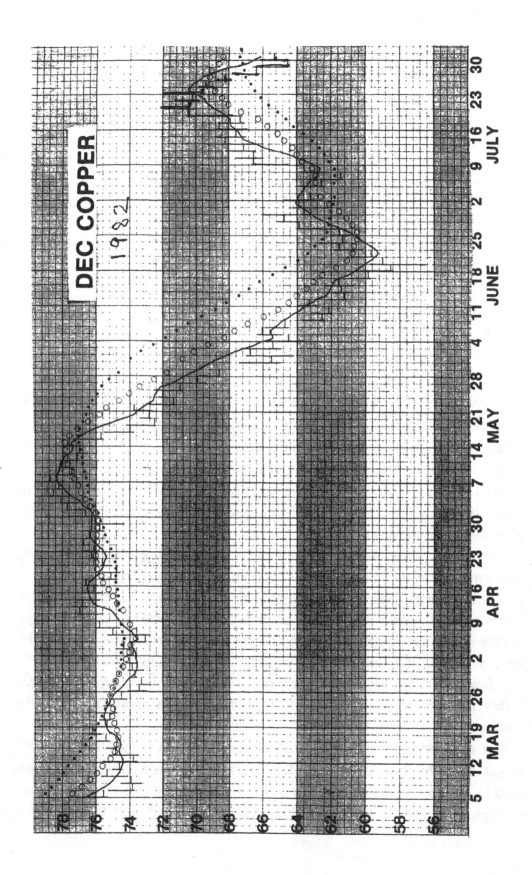

DEC COPPER

1982

and go lightly "short".

In other words, use only ⅓ of the equity in your account.

At the end of that day, the 9 day average should be moving up close to the 4 day average. This indicates that the "bullish" momentum of the past few weeks or months is slowing down.

But—remember that, if prices continue to sell above the 18 day average, you cannot go "safely short" or be heavily committed to the short side of the market. The reason is—

A MAJOR, SUSTAINED AND PROFITABLE MOVE DOWN CANNOT OCCUR UNTIL PRICES CLOSE BELOW THE 18 DAY AVERAGE

This can be seen by looking at the charts in the long and sustained bear markets in so many of the commodities during their long declines during the year 1982. A few charts given in this book will illustrate that point.

As soon as prices move down to a point where they are definitely below the 4 day and the 9 day averages, you can then sell "short" some more contracts equal to about the same number as your original "short sales", which was based on using only ⅓ of the capital in your account. At this point, you are now using about ⅔ of your capital.

Finally—before the close of the day that prices move down to or near the point where they will definitely be below the 18 day average—sell some more contracts "short" for the "breakout move" that, in most commodities, will then begin to pick up speed as prices move lower at a faster rate.

A new bear market will then develop and last from three weeks to three months and, possibly, more. After this decline has taken place, a larger amount of "bearish news" will gradually and persistently be made known. This will be in contrast to the "bullish news" that was given out only a few weeks earlier.

After the decline in price gets underway, this more definite "bearish" trend will provide you with very large profits on the original contracts you sold near the top, a good profit on the second group of contracts you sold

61

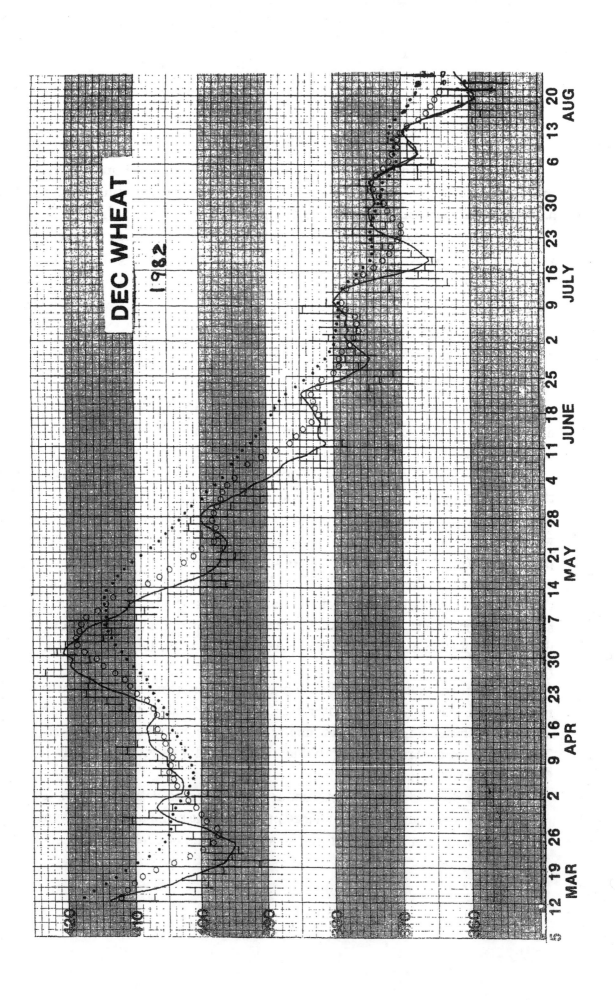

after the top was made and a good potential for profit on the last group of contracts you sold as the market finally indicates it would continue to move down towards a lower level.

You must, then, hold your short positions until the 4, 9 and 18 day average confirms a new uptrend.

Note—While the above plan will give you very large profits—on a comparatively safe basis—it will not assure you of large profits EVERYTIME you use that rule.

Why?

Because NO RULE in commodities is perfect—as pointed out on the previous pages. Occasionally, there are "traps" and a "bear trap" could occur soon after the "breakout" and the decline begins.

Then, instead of continuing to move lower, that market may turn around, for some reason, then move up and "trap" the "shorts" who felt they were right in selling, but found that the market decided, for some reason, to move higher instead of lower. (See the charts marked with the words "bear trap" or "bull trap").

The truth is—it still requires good judgment to know when a major trend is reversing or has reversed enough to cause the beginning of a new trend in the opposite direction.

In brief—the R. C. Allen version of the "moving averages" help you to be "right" in the market at least 80% of the time. This means you are, generally, in the market on the right side at least 8 out of 10 major UP moves and 8 out of 10 major DOWN moves—and that is where the largest profits are always made.

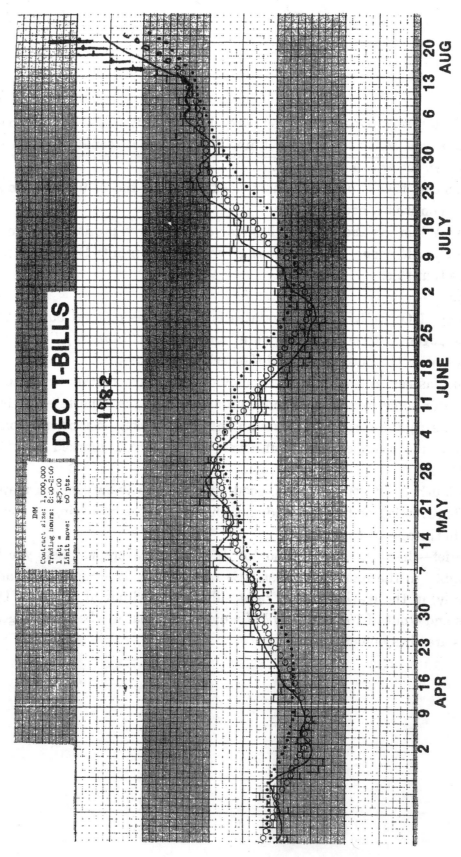

DEC T-BILLS

1982

IMM
Contract size: 1,000,000
Trading hours: 8:00-2:00
1 pt = $25.00
Limit move: 60 pts.

APR 2 9 16 23 30 MAY 7 14 21 28 JUNE 4 11 18 25 JULY 2 9 16 23 30 AUG 6 13 20

64

11

HOW THIS PROFESSIONAL SYSTEM CAN
SAVE YOU BOTH TIME AND MONEY

The reason why the "moving averages" can save you both time and money is—all of the news, opinions, open-interest figures and the volume of sales are considered, digested and discussed at tops and bottoms and the slow changing opinions from bullish to bearish (near the top of a market) and the slow changing opinions from bearish to bullish (near the bottom), eventually make themselves known, over a period of several days to several weeks.

As those shifts of opinion occur, the 4 day average slows down. The 9 day average moves closer to the 4 day average. This gives further cause to believe that the trend may be definitely changing.

This saves you time because you do not have to do all the figuring necessary to determine the change in trend. And it will save you money because you will enter the market—either long or short—on a much safer basis.

If the 4 day average and the 9 day average both slow down, the 18 day average will then catch up rapidly—possibly in only a few more days.

If you are long and prices finally sell below all three averages, the next trend will be down for at least 10 days to three weeks. And in a major long-term down trend, prices may continue to move lower for six weeks to several months.

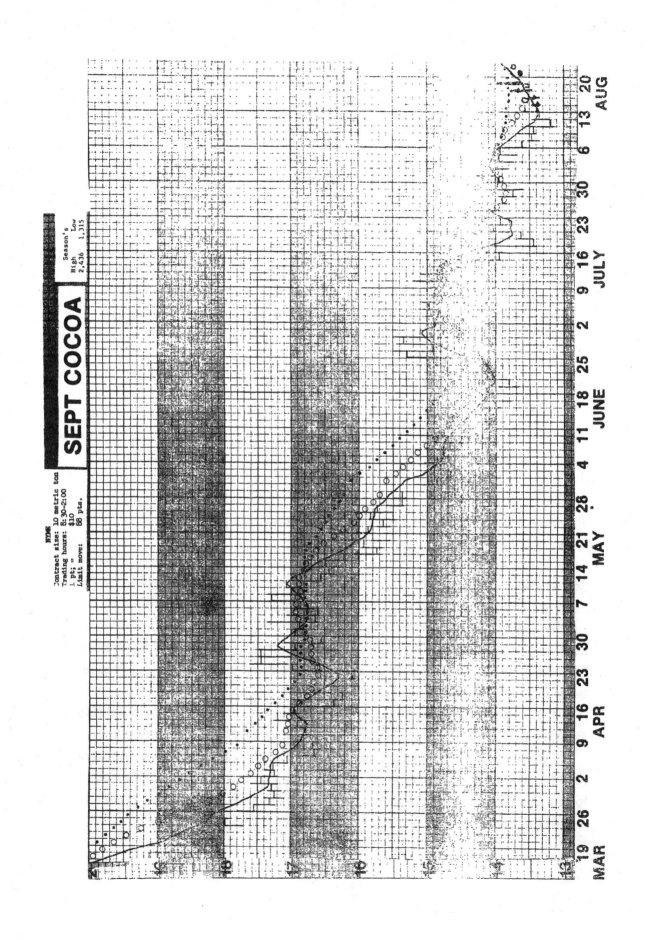

SEPT COCOA

NYME

Contract size: 10 metric ton
Trading hours: 8:30-2:00
1 pt; = $10
Limit move: 88 pts.

Season's
High   Low
2,436   1,315

Over the years, there have been many bear markets that have lasted for seven to ten months without any change in trend.

If you are short and prices continue to decline for that length of time—your profits, obviously, will be very large. And that is the reason why, earlier in this book, I pointed out the importance of looking for ways to earn those large profits.

Many of the charts in this book illustrate how much profit can be earned from only one contract by observing the 4, 9 and 18 day moving averages—even though you fail to sell "at the top" and fail to buy "near the bottom".

If you trade in two or more contracts, you can easily see that your profits, each year, can be tremendous—possibly 500% to 800% or more.

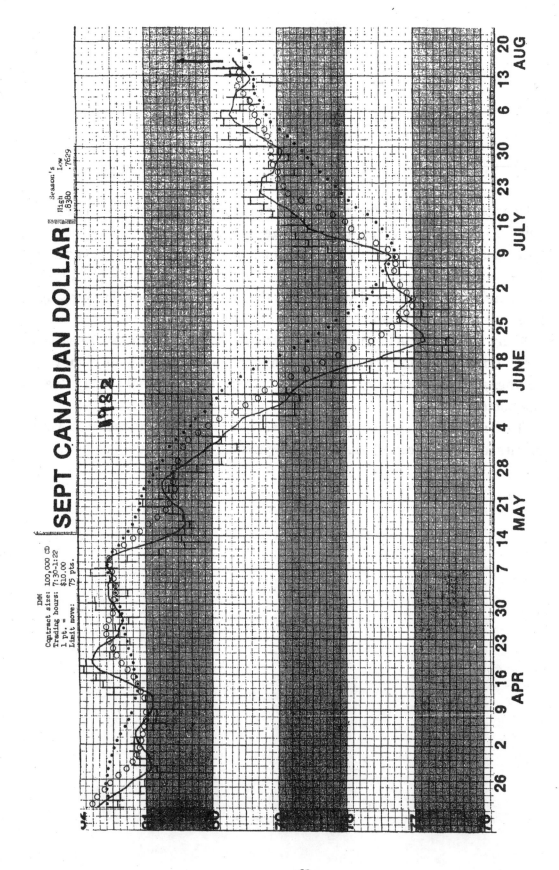

SEPT CANADIAN DOLLAR

1982

IMM
Contract size: 100,000 CD
Trading hours: 7:30-1:22
1 pt. = $10.00
Limit move: 75 pts.

Season's
High   Low
.8380 .7629

12

MOVING AVERAGES
AGAINST THE FUNDAMENTALS

A criticism you may hear concerning the "moving averages" is—"This trading technique seems to substitute a mechanical system for fundamental judgment."

But, the truth is—those who try to use judgment, based on the fundamentals alone, are inclined, too often, to miss the major trends as soon as they begin to make their change—UP or DOWN.

Instead, they are inclined to hold on too long to a losing position because their "judgment" has not, yet, been proven wrong.

As the market moves against them, they, eventually, see why they should have made a decision to "reverse their position" much sooner.

Since this is so often true—how can most traders know how to buy or sell for the largest profits possible?

Part of the answer is to learn more about the fundamentals. Page 38 of the book—HOW TO BUILD A FORTUNE IN COMMODITIES— points out that—when prices are high—the good news is well-known. The large commercial interests in that commodity discount that news. They place "short hedges" because they believe that, within a few more days, the news will not be so bullish.

From those high prices, a decline will set in and prices will then move lower until those lower prices will justify the bearish news for that commodity that will be made known as prices make a bottom.

When prices are low—the bad news you hear or read about will soon be overcome by a slow, but steady increase in more favorable news until prices, once again, reach a level where those higher prices will justify the good news that will be made known as prices reach their "top".

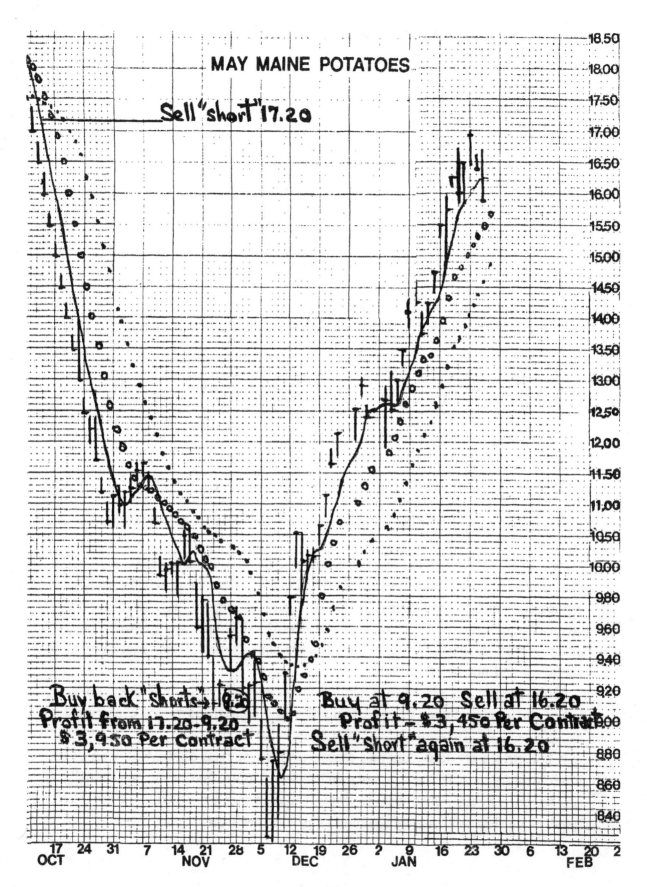

MAY MAINE POTATOES

Sell "short" 17.20

Buy back "shorts" @ 9.20
Profit from 17.20-9.20
$3,950 Per Contract

Buy at 9.20 Sell at 16.20
Profit - $3,450 Per Contract
Sell "short" again at 16.20

| 17 | 24 | 31 | 7 | 14 | 21 | 28 | 5 | 12 | 19 | 26 | 2 | 9 | 16 | 23 | 30 | 6 | 13 | 20 | 2 |
OCT   NOV   DEC   JAN   FEB

70

A copy of Page 38 from the book—HOW TO BUILD A FORTUNE IN COMMODITIES—is reprinted below to give you a more visual picture of how all markets, eventually, follow what the fundamentals will be—IN THE FUTURE.

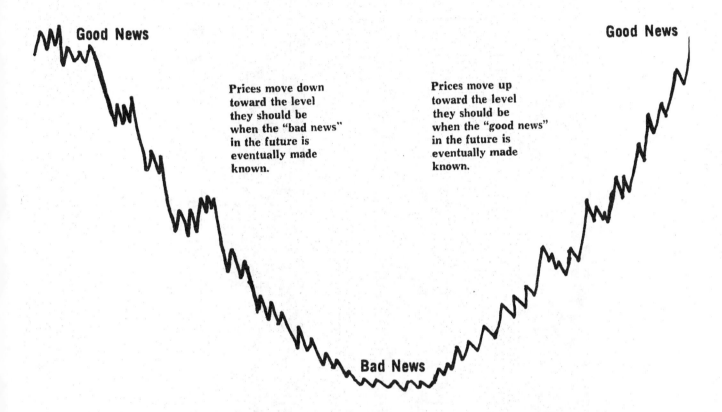

Good News

Prices move down toward the level they should be when the "bad news" in the future is eventually made known.

Prices move up toward the level they should be when the "good news" in the future is eventually made known.

Good News

Bad News

For those traders who like to "pick the top" of a move, the 4, 9 and 18 day moving averages can give you a fairly good spot to place "short sales" close to that top.

But, if you sell short before the moving averages give you a positive "signal" that a long-term decline will soon occur, then that top may prove to be only a temporary resistance in a long-term bull market. Prices may then move up and make a new top somewhat higher.

You must, therefore, make certain you enter an order to "buy on a stop" at a price just a little BELOW the highest price made a few days earlier on the previous UP move.

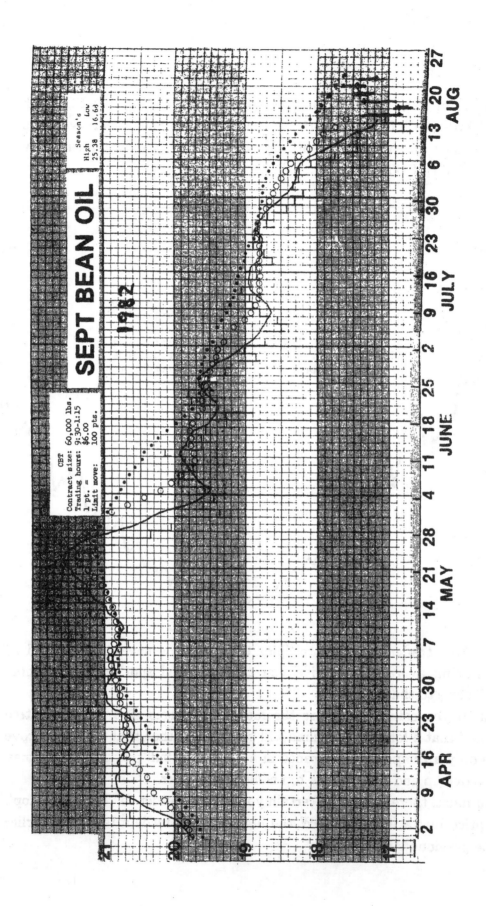

SEPT BEAN OIL

1982

CBT
Contract size: 60,000 lbs.
Trading hours: 9:30-1:15
1 pt. = $6.00
Limit move: 100 pts.

Season's
High   Low
25.38   16.68

If prices actually do move higher, instead of lower, you will then be out of your "short sales" with a small loss and you will automatically have a new "long" position at that point where you had an order to "buy on a stop".

You will see the reason for that new long position, more clearly, on the many charts given in this book. Then you will know why trying to "pick a top" without considering the "moving averages"—especially the 18 day average—is a very risky business.

That is why you should have patience and not buy or sell prematurely. Instead, wait for some more definite "signal".

If, at any time, you should be wrong, get out of your position immediately before a small loss turns into a greater loss as that market continues to move against you.

Since the 4 day average is just an alert signal to indicate that, possibly, a top is being made, you must then consider how the 9 day average is moving. As a general rule, in a bull market, the 9 day average will move higher, at a slower pace than the 4 day average because more daily closing prices are used to get that 9 day average.

When prices are low and completing a "bottom", the same principle concerning the action of prices at a top should also be considered when prices are making that bottom.

In brief, you should watch the 4 day average very closely because the 4 day average is a "signal" that can alert you to a possible change in trend from DOWN to UP. But you must remember that the trend will not be definitely and safely "bullish" until prices have closed at or near the 18 day average.

Until prices do close at or near the 18 day average, all rallies that occur from any new low, must be treated as a "bear market rally"—not as the beginning of a new "bull market."

This means that, instead of planning to be definitely "long" as that rally begins, you should, instead, plan to "sell short" once again and try to buy at a lower level.

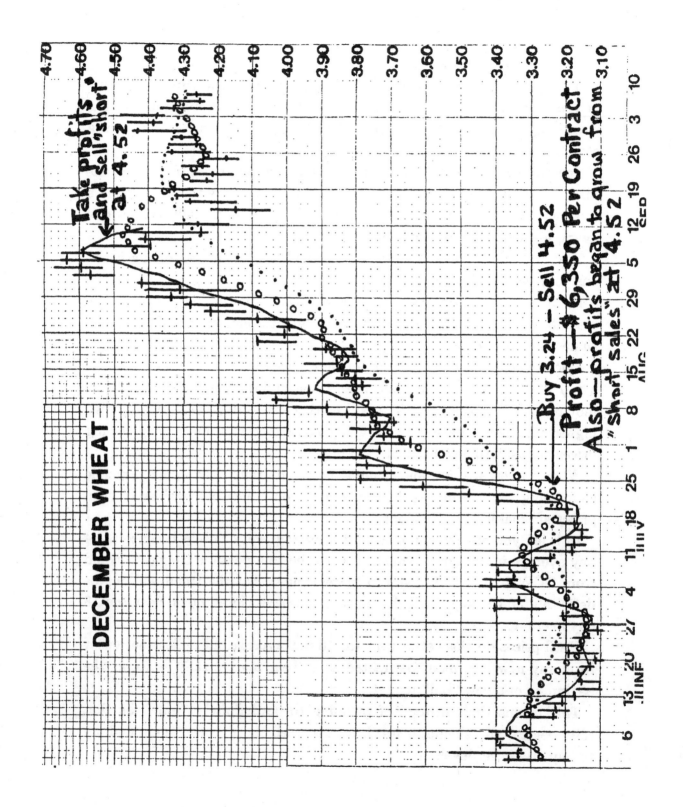

DECEMBER WHEAT

Take Profits
and Sell "short"
at 4.52

Buy 3.24 — Sell 4.52
Profit — $6,350 Per Contract
Also — Profits began to grow from
"short sales" at 4.52

Unfortunately, however, many commodity markets, quite often, will get into indecisive, "trading markets" that will last for several weeks and, occasionally, they will last for several months.

This means—there will be several interruptions in each UP trend (bull market) and several interruptions in every DOWN trend (bear market). These interruptions or "trading markets" tend to cause the majority of traders some concern.

They find it difficult to determine whether the UP move or the DOWN move will continue. This uncertainty causes prices to fluctuate indecisively within that general trading range. This erratic movement confuses traders and many of them experience many losses as they are "whipsawed" in and out of trades.

Some solutions to those problems will be given later in this book so you will understand, more clearly, how to protect yourself and plan your strategy during those indecisive, trading markets.

THE MAJORITY OF TRADERS MAKE MISTAKES

Fortunately for you—the majority of traders make mistakes. Some of the reasons why were given earlier and they continue to make those mistakes, month after month, year after year. This means they will eventually lose money.

Obviously, if the majority of traders lose money, then you, as one of the more professional traders, can earn a large amount of money when you are right.

The majority of traders lose money for one or more of the three following reasons—

      1. They don't know WHICH commodity to buy or
      sell so they buy or sell the commodity they have heard
      a lot about—or one in which some friend or broker
      has an interest and he joins them.

      2. They don't know WHAT TIME to buy or sell. In

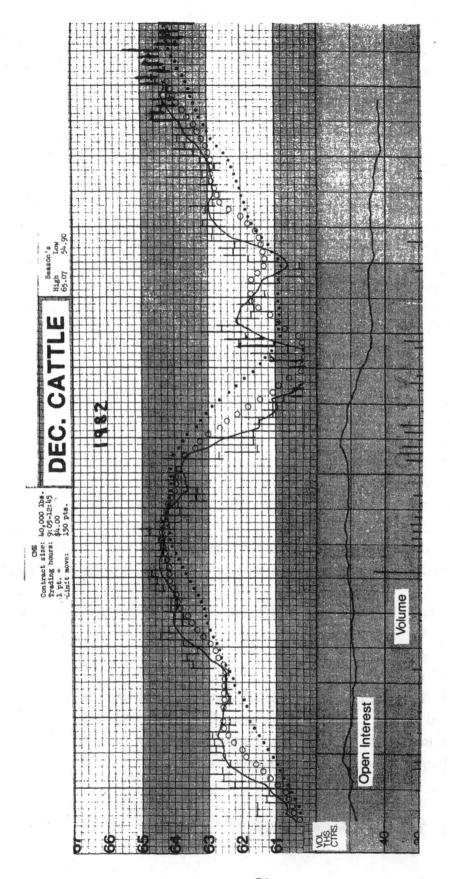

DEC. CATTLE

Season's
High   Low
65.07   54.90

CME
Contract size: 40,000 lbs.
Trading hours: 9:05-12:45
1 pt. = $4.00
limit move: 150 pts.

1982

Open Interest

Volume

VOL.
THS.
CTRS.

66
65
64
63
62
61

40

this case, they may be influenced by a friend or broker who may have bought or sold too soon. They find out, too late, that their friend or broker was right—at the wrong time.

3. They fail to control their emotions. Too often, they let "hope" or fear or greed enter their minds. This causes them to act in a way that a little more study and analysis would induce them to say, "I shouldn't have done that."

And, at times, they get hard-headed. They hold on to a losing position too long. (Even the best of professional traders do this occasionally.)

Instead of being flexible, they may stay with a losing trade—even though they are wrong. Then, they may put up some more money, hold on and try to "fight it out."

Their pride and their ego will not allow them to say, "I was wrong. I must get out."

Because the above is true—you may find it is wise to be a "lone wolf". And if you know how to use the "moving averages" as I explain them in this book, you can be a lone wolf and be, in most cases, very successful.

This means—you will find it is wise to keep your trading plans a secret. Don't tell anyone what you plan to do—not even your broker. And, above all, you must ignore the "advice" and the opinions expressed by customers who sit in broker's offices. Most of them will confuse you.

Such boardroom traders usually trade on "hopes" and "wishes". And very few of them make money. They are too close to the market to see the big moves that are beginning to develop.

The truth is—there are no rich traders sitting around in board rooms. Most of those who did sit there have gone broke. And that is true because brokerage offices are confusing places to be.

That is true because brokers tend to have an opinion or belief about a certain market and tend to induce their customers to follow them. It may

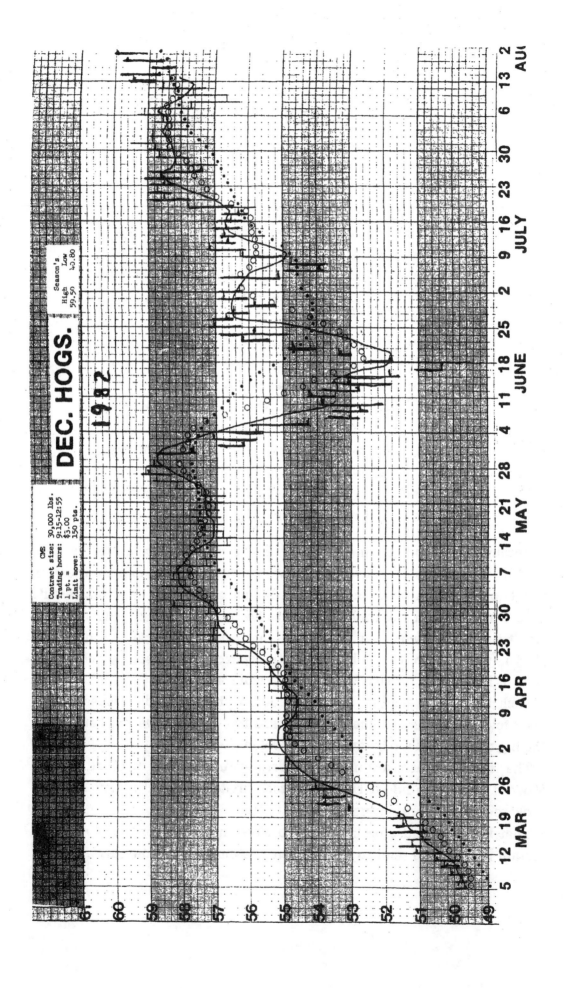

DEC. HOGS.

1982

CME

Contract size: 30,000 lbs.
Trading hours: 9:15-12:55
1 pt. = $3.00
Limit move: 150 pts.

Season's
High   Low
59.50   40.80

take several weeks of large losses before those brokers will be convinced they were wrong.

Of course, other brokers, in the same office, may have an opposite opinion. So, at the same time, they will help to make their customers some money.

At another time, the first broker will be right and the opinions of the second broker will be wrong.

Now you can see the reason why it was so necessary for me to originate and develop a *Professional Trading System* based upon the "moving averages".

If you follow the ideas and the rules in this book, you could live one thousand miles from the nearest brokerage office, trade in carefully selected "special situations" only once or twice each month and, if you are properly margined, you can take large profits from many of your trades—enough, in fact, to earn 300% or more—every year.

All you need to do is—observe the changes in trends as they develop on your "moving averages" charts. This means—you should BUY at the time when the market indicates a definite turn from DOWN to UP or SELL at the time when the market indicates a definite turn from UP to DOWN.

The many charts in this book will help you understand the turns that occur so often each year.

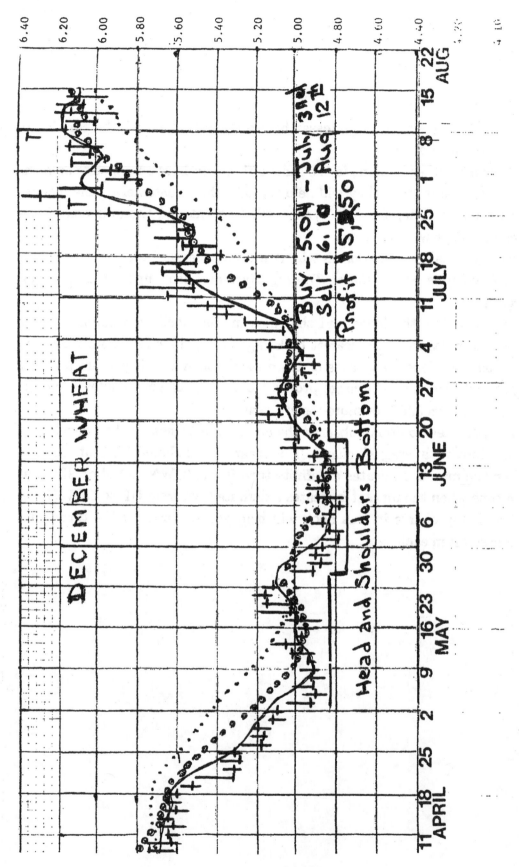

DECEMBER WHEAT

Buy — 5.04 — July 3rd
Sell — 6.10 — Aug 12th

Profit $5,250

Head and Shoulders Bottom

80

When the 4 day average and the 9 day average meet, the market may then reverse itself—especially if the 18 day average has moved far enough to indicate that, within another day or two, the 4 day average and the 9 day average may close at a price near the 18 day average. When that occurs, the following may be true.

IF THE LAST MAJOR MOVE OF FIVE WEEKS OR MORE
WAS UP
THE NEXT MAJOR MOVE MAY BE DOWN
IF THE LAST MAJOR MOVE OF FIVE WEEKS OR MORE
WAS DOWN
THE NEXT MAJOR MOVE MAY BE UP

A few examples of such tops and bottoms are given in the charts in this book. After you check those charts and make some notes, you will, then, understand, more clearly, why you can earn a larger amount of money, in the majority of cases, when you follow the 4 day, 9 day and the 18 day moving averages.

As pointed out earlier in this book, there is NO PERFECT SYSTEM for beating the commodity market. So you must always plan to take the largest profits possible to offset the many small losses you will have to take from time to time.

FINAL TOPS

Before the start of a new "bear market", an area develops where "longs" who have large profits are willing to sell to new buyers or to "shorts" who have to buy to protect themselves against the fear of further losses.

These new buy orders help to keep prices at a high level—sometimes for several weeks if the general mood is quite bullish.

If, however, prices rose rapidly—almost straight up—the decline may then be just as fast—almost straight down.

Prices may drop rapidly to a level where enough buyers are willing, once again, to enter the market on the long side. But their purchases are generally made in "hopes" they can catch a sharp "bear market rally" that could carry prices up a point just below the previous highs.

The charts below show how some commodities act and react during periods when a final top is being made. Such areas occur when a commodity is being passed from strong hands over to the weak hands of individuals who seldom buy unless they feel the news is bullish.

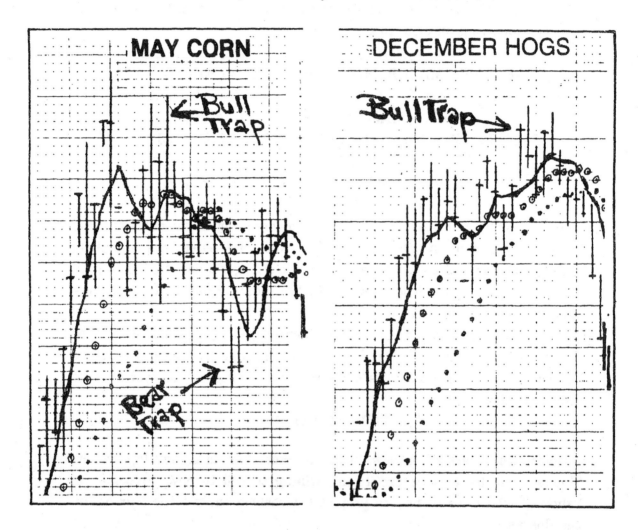

The new buyers, unfortunately, cannot support the market against the steady "pressure" put on by sales by the "professionals" and the large amount of "short hedges" put on by the big commercial companies who must put on those "short hedges" to protect themselves against a possible decline in price.

As new lows are made, those "weak longs" are forced to sell out their long positions. Otherwise they will have to suffer continuously larger losses as prices move lower.

13

CHART PATTERNS
YOU CAN, GENERALLY, RELY ON

AREAS OF MINOR DISTRIBUTION
AS PRICES MOVE LOWER

After a "bear market" gets underway, it takes time for prices to move down far enough to create a good base for the next bull move—just as it takes time for prices in a "bull market" to move high enough to create a top where short sales can be made with some degree of assurance that the final top has been made.

You will find that, after a good decline of several days to several weeks, prices will stop moving lower and work into a "trading range" for a few days to a few weeks. During that "trading range", prices will quite often, create patterns that may look a bit like "triangles" or "pennants".

After a period of several days to a few weeks, indications will be given that will give you enough confidence to sell more contracts "short".

The temporary strength of the market during the time spent within that "triangle" or "pennant" soon dissipates, prices will then break out on the downside and decline to a level where new lows are recorded.

The 18 day average will act as a sort of guide and it will seem to guide prices lower.

The illustration below will give you an idea of how these declines and areas of consolidation appear during a "bear market".

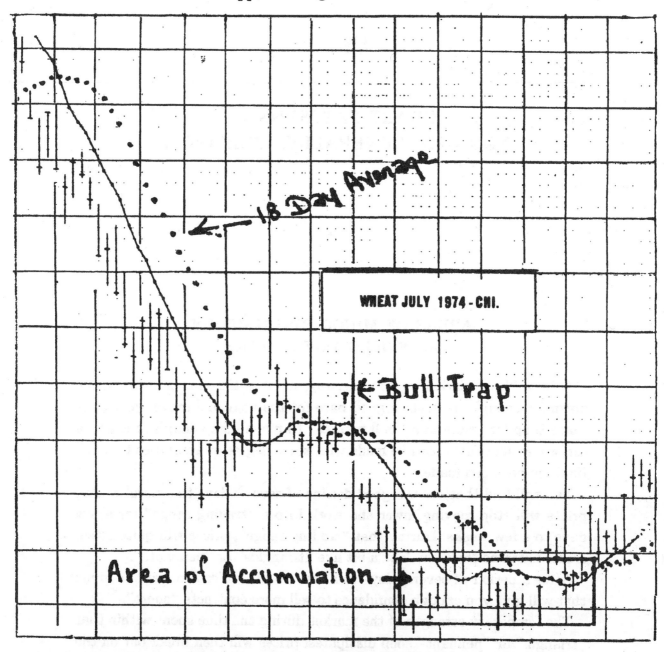

Not all commodities have the same type of bear market formations, but the principles are the same. Each decline will have an area of consolidation before the next decline begins. And there may be three to five areas of consolidation before a new "bottom" is formed. This will create the base that is needed for the next "bull market".

FINAL BOTTOMS

These are areas where "shorts" who have large profits from the recent downward moves are now willing to buy back those "shorts". And many of them will decide, at that time, to go lightly long.

Prices, however, remain at a low level due to new "short sales" and liquidation by "weak longs" who are inclined to sell because the "news" they hear is so bearish.

Professional traders, however, now feel more confident that a bottom is being made. They are, therefore, willing to take a "long position" in anticipation of the next bull move.

In addition, orders by the large companies with a commercial interest in that commodity help to cause a slow-down in the "bearish" momentum and those orders to buy give support and they add stability to the market around that level.

This is marked—AREA OF ACCUMULATION—on the opposite page.

BOTTOMS FOR THE BEGINNING OF A BULL MOVE

When a bottom is being formed for a new bull move, a few false starts may occur before prices will begin a definite move UP towards higher levels. And, quite often, a "bear trap" will occur a few days before prices break out above that area of congestion.

The "bear trap" comes after one last bit of "bearish news" that causes "weak longs" to get out because they "fear" that prices may, once again, move lower.

See the areas marked "bear trap" that are marked on many of the charts in this book.

"Bear traps" occur for the same general reason that "bull traps" occur. Fear and lack patience. Traders who see prices are at a low level due to "bearish news" are inclined to give too much attention and importance to that "news". And, if more bearish news is given out, they are likely to "sell short" due to that bearish news.

A few days later, the market turns around and moves higher. Those "bears" who sincerely believed that "bearish news" are then caught "short". If they do not get out of their "short positions"—immediately—take their loss and then go long—they may find that most of their capital will soon be lost as the market continues to move against them—especially if the charts indicate that prices are definitely trading above the 18 day averages.

In such a case, you should never be "short" when the bull move starts because prices may continue to trend higher until they make a top close to or even above the area of the previous top.

The July Soybean Meal chart below illustrates how a potentially profitable bear market may be followed by watching the 4 day, 9 day and 18 day moving averages.

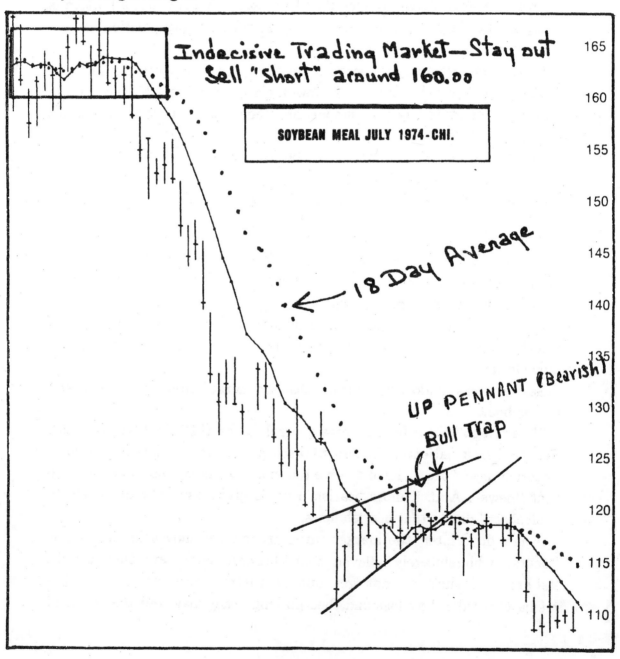

The profit from the "short sale" at 160.00 down to a point where those "short sales" can be bought back near the bottom around 115.00 is 45 points. That is a profit of $4,500 per contract in only seven weeks.

Such profit potentials will often occur in many different commodities sometimes as often as twice each year. Some will occur in "bear markets". Others will occur in "bull markets".

Occasionally, you may find a "bull trap" will develop in many bear markets. (One is illustrated on the chart of the July Soybean Meal). But, if a bull trap occurs after an UP PENNANT forms, then you can hold your short position because an UP PENNANT indicates that the next move will be DOWN.

The rule concerning UP PENNANTS will help you stay in that potential "short position". Or, you can safely "sell short" before prices break out on the downside of that UP PENNANT.

This is especially true if the closing prices are definitely below the 18 day averages.

TRADING MARKETS

Trading markets are consolidation areas. They occur because traders are not certain which way the next move will be. They usually create patterns called "triangles" or "pennants".

In bull markets, they will occur because—after a rise in price, a large amount of supply of that commodity comes on the market. This will, temporarily, slow down the rise in price as that supply is distributed and absorbed by buyers who are willing to pay that higher price—at that time.

And, in bear markets, they occur because—after a decline in price, new orders to buy at that lower price will cause the market to hesitate for several days to several weeks. Then, as an increasing supply of that commodity becomes available, buyers tend to back away from the market.

Instead of continuing to buy, they will tend to wait and hope to buy at lower prices due to that increase in the supply.

If a bull market is to continue to move towards higher levels, an increasing amount of demand must come from those traders who are willing to buy and absorb all those sales that are being offered.

After several days and, occasionally, after several weeks of trading, the supply at that level will slowly dry up. New buyers will then have to enter orders to buy—at higher prices—in order to secure the contracts they need.

Owners of the actual cash commodity then begin to hold back further sales at that price level in hopes that they can sell that commodity at higher prices.

The demand then picks up enough to overcome the small supply. Prices then move up to a higher level once again.

Generally, a bull market will make a top after there have been AT LEAST THREE of those trading range (consolidation) areas. Occasionally, in a strong bull market, there will be four of those trading areas. Very seldom will you find FIVE except in a very strong bull market.

On a long-term chart, those consolidation areas and tops will usually form a pattern similar to those illustrated below.

Bear markets will usually be exactly the reverse.

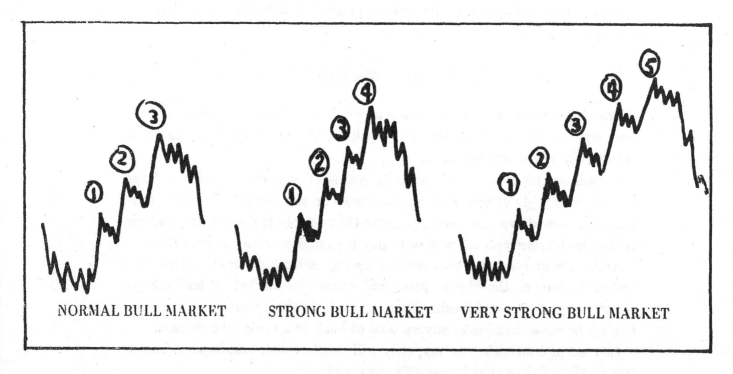

NORMAL BULL MARKET   STRONG BULL MARKET   VERY STRONG BULL MARKET

TRIANGLES AND PENNANTS WITH BULLISH POTENTIALS

In a bull market—three types of triangles and pennants develop. The longer the time it takes to build the triangle or pennant, the more certain the move will be when the breakout to new highs begins.

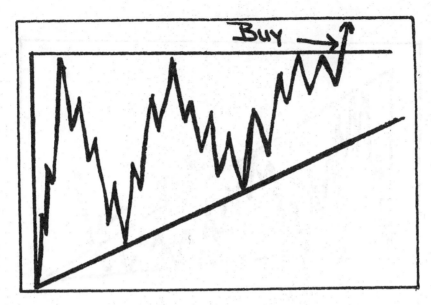

1. An ascending triangle with a breakout on the upside. When prices reach a point where they will definitely move above the top line of the triangle, you must then enter an order to "buy at the market" regardless of price because, at that time, all of the important forces in the market are convinced that prices will be moving higher.

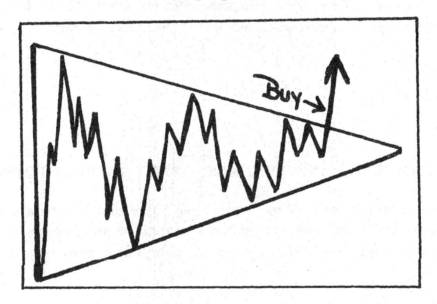

2. A perfect triangle with a breakout on the upside. When prices reach a point where they will definitely move above the top line of the triangle, you must, then, enter an order to "buy at the market" because all of the indecision and uncertainty has been removed and those who know most about the potential for that market, know that prices will soon be moving higher.

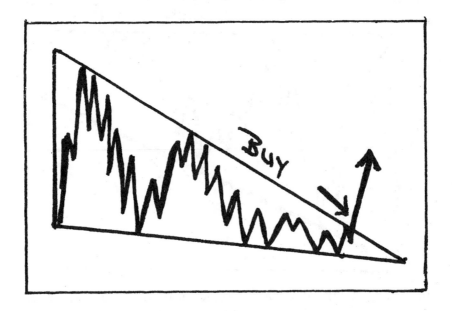

3. A descending triangle—or—DOWN PENNANT—with a breakout on the upside. When prices reach a point where they will definitely move above the top line of the triangle, you must, then enter an order to "buy at the market". Further confirmation that the trend will be persistently UP will be given when prices close above the 18 day average.

TRIANGLES AND PENNANTS WITH BEARISH POTENTIALS

In a bear market—three types of triangles and pennants develop. The longer the time it takes to build the triangle or pennant, the more certain the move will be when the breakout to new lows begins.

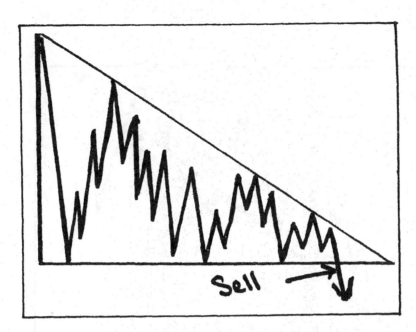

1.   A descending triangle with a breakout on the downside. When prices reach a point where they will definitely move below the bottom line of the triangle, you must, then, enter an order to "sell at the market" regardless of price because at that time, all of the important forces in the market are convinced that prices will be moving lower.

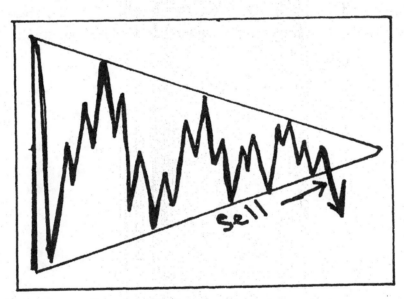

2.   A perfect triangle with a breakout on the downside. When prices reach a point where they will definitely move below the bottom line of that triangle—you must, then, enter an order to "sell at the market" because all of the indecision and uncertainty has been removed and those who know most about the potential for that market, know that prices will soon be moving lower.

91

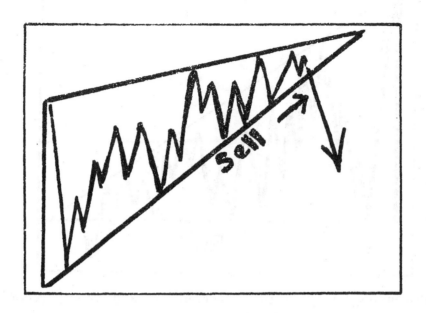

3.   An ascending triangle—or—UP PENNANT—with a breakout on the downside. When prices reach a point where they will definitely break below the bottom of this UP triangle or pennant, you must, then, enter an order to "sell at the market". Further confirmation that the trend will be persistently DOWN will be given when prices close below the 18 day average.

14

SOME RULES PROFESSIONALS FOLLOW

It is difficult for business men to make money in commodities because they expect commodity markets to act in a logical, business-like manner. They do not realize that commodity markets will always move UP or DOWN to a price level where the market will be accurate and justified—in the future.

That fact—in the future—is the most difficult for most traders to understand. And, until they understand and trade according to what prices will be—in the future—the majority of them will always lose money.

Professionals, however, are a bit more realistic. And there are some general rules they follow that help them earn more money than those who do not take the time to become more professional in their trading.

Below are some rules the majority of professionals understand and follow. As you read over these rules, you will begin to understand why the 4, 9 and 18 day average will help you earn more money in the commodity markets in spite of the confusion those markets create for so many of those who trade.

1. Never fall in love with any commodity. Continuously re-evaluate each market and, most important, look for those commodities that seem to offer a "special situation". (See the chapter on "Special Situations—the Key to Profits." in the book—HOW TO BUILD A FORTUNE IN COMMODITIES).

This book points out that a "special situation" indicates the possibility that prices may move far enough to earn a large profit—at least 100% or more over a period of several weeks.

This will, of course, help you to stay out of the indecisive, time-wasting and usually unprofitable "trading markets" that occur, so often, every year.

2. If, at any time, you take a position and it proves to be wrong, you should make certain you get out of that position before your losses grow larger. Then, after you have gotten out of that position, wait—at least two full days before you enter that market again.

If you were "short" and the market went up, you will usually find that at the end of that time (two days), you can sell that commodity "short" once again at a higher price than you sold it two days earlier.

And, if you happened to get out of a "long" position, but the market declined, you can buy that same commodity once again at a lower price.

3. Always follow the TREND indicated by the "moving averages". This means you must never stubbornly hold onto a losing position if the "moving averages" as discussed in this book says, "You are wrong."

A day or two later, some type of news will be released that will give some reason "why" the market moved in the direction it did.

4. Bullish or bearish news is never given out near the bottom or the top of a move. Instead, such bullish or bearish news will be given out only after the actual move is well underway.

That is why it is so important to watch the "moving averages" and follow the TREND so you can BUY or SELL before the news comes out.

5. Markets very seldom move straight up or straight down. Instead, prices of most commodities tend to spend more days every year trading in areas of congestion (commonly called "trading markets") than the number of days they spend in a definite move UP or a definite move DOWN.

6. In a "bull market," buy the second nearest option, then follow the move up as prices continue to move higher. (The second nearest option means—if March is the nearest option, trade in May. If July is the nearest, trade in August. If October is the nearest option, trade in November, and so on.)

7. In the case of "bear markets", sell the nearest option "short".

8. During areas of consolidation (when triangles or pennants are often created), prices will, generally, remain above the 18 day average.

The exceptions will be the "bull traps" and the "bear traps" which occur, occasionally in many commodities.

That is why (1) no rule is perfect when trading in commodities (2) you must always be alert and (3) you must take small losses—if you happen to be wrong.

Several charts are included in this book with "bull traps" and "bear traps" marked on those charts. Look at them carefully and remember to get out of a "trap" quickly—if you happen to be "suckered" into that "trap" by news or rumors.

9. When the prices for two or three days close at or near the 4 day average, take your profits. Buy back your "short" position if you are short—or—sell and take your profits if you are long. Then, stay out of the market for at least one or two days. (In other words, you should obey Rule 25 in Chapter 10 of the book—HOW TO BUILD A FORTUNE IN COMMODITIES).

10. Now—watch the 9 day average very closely. If the 9 day average is moving down close to the 4 day average—it indicates that a bottom may soon be made.

At this point—use one-third (⅓) of the money in your margin account and take a long position. Do not use more than ⅓ of your margin at this time because prices could remain at a low level for a few more days and, possibly, for a few more weeks.

11. Now—watch the 18 day average. If prices look like they will close at or close to the 18 day average and those prices are trading above the 4 day and the 9 day average, then use another ⅓ of your margin to take another long position.

Then, the first day that price moves above the 4 day, 9 day and the 18 day average, use the remaining ⅓ of your margin to take another long position.

12. Now—you will have three long positions with an average close to the bottom of the move. (Remember that—no one can buy at the bottom—and no one knows exactly where a bottom may be.)

Stay with those long positions until prices move sharply higher and until they give an indication that a top may be near.

This move towards higher prices may last from two weeks to several months so do not be in any hurry to take profits—especially if prices are trading above the 18 day average. (Read page 55 and 56 once again.)

13. In every strong bull move, there will be declines of from one and one-half days to three days. Don't let those declines scare you out of your long positions—especially if prices close above the 18 day average.

In fact—you should try to buy another contract after prices have declined those one-and one-half to three days—especially if the next closing price is higher than the last closing price.

This is one of the safest and most reliable ways to pyramid your profits.

14. Now—get ready to determine the best price to sell near the top of that bull move. You can do this by going over the principles concerning the 4 day, the 9 day and the 18 day averages.

15. The best time to take profits and sell "short" is—after a long rise of several weeks to several months. The "news" will be bullish. Most of the smaller traders will be inclined to buy. But remember my point earlier in this book—90% of the traders are usually wrong and they have to lose a large amount of money—before the 10% of traders who are right can earn a large amount of money.

Prices at that high level will seem to be "strong". The 9 day average will then continue to move higher and soon will meet the 4 day average. When you see that is occuring, try to sell "short" one hour before the close on the day when the closing price for that day is likely to be either at or below the 4 day and the 9 day average.

16. At that point in time, the 18 day average will continue to move up towards the 4 day and the 9 day average. If you happen to be "short" only a few contracts and the market seems to be moving in your favor, you can then sell more contracts "short" with greater confidence the day

that the 4 day and the 9 day averages CLOSE at a price NEAR or BELOW the 18 day average. (See the many charts in this book).

As prices begin their downward move and create a new major bear market, there will be areas of consolidation on each decline (usually Triangles or Pennants where prices will move up and down in a comparatively narrow range for a few days and—sometimes—for a few weeks). Such Triangles and Pennants create more opportunities to sell additional contracts "short" before prices break out and decline to make new option lows.

17.   Remember that no rule is perfect because people and markets are not perfect. If there were perfect, infallible rules, then everyone who followed those rules would soon be rich.

All rules in commodity trading are, therefore, simply guides that may work approximately 70% of the time. That is one of the reasons why "stop losses" are so important. Such "stop losses" will help to protect you against the large losses that may occur during the 30% of the time when you may be wrong.